Finding our familia

The story of our children adopted from overseas

STEVAN WHITEHEAD

AF

DOPTION
OSTERING

Published by
British Association for Adoption & Fostering
(BAAF)
Saffron House
6–10 Kirby Street
London EC1N 8TS
www.baaf.org.uk

Charity registration 275689 (England & Wales)
and SC039337 (Scotland)

British Library Cataloguing in Publication Data
A catalogue record for this book is available from
the British Library

ISBN 978 1 907585 52 4

Cover design by Helen Joubert
Designed by Andrew Haig & Associates
Typeset by Fravashi Aga
Printed in Great Britain by T J International
Trade distribution by Turnaround Publisher Services, Unit 3,
Olympia Trading Estate, Coburg Road, London N22 6TZ

BAAF is the leading UK-wide membership organisation for all
those concerned with adoption, fostering and child care issues.

The paper used for the text pages of this book is FSC certified.
FSC (The Forest Stewardship Council) is an international network
to promote responsible management of the world's forests.

Printed on totally chlorine-free paper.

FSC
www.fsc.org
MIX
Paper from
responsible sources
FSC® C013056

Contents

Acknowledgements

Thanks to the British Association for Adoption and Fostering for publishing our story and to Hedi for her generosity and understanding. Thanks also to Peter Selman for all his work with both BAAF and the Network for Intercountry Adoption – and especially for giving us access to his huge store of knowledge and wisdom.

I have to say a huge thank you to my family for letting me share our story and to our familia for allowing it to happen.

Finally, I would like to say how grateful I am to all the members of the intercountry adoption community here and around the world for their support, understanding and generosity of spirit, without which we would not be where we are, or be heading where we are going.

All the positives come from others – all the errors are entirely my own.

About the author

Stevan was born in Oxford and has lived and worked around the world. He worked for thirty years in Marketing and Communications before moving on to building a new career in property.

Stevan has been actively involved in both intercountry and domestic adoption in the UK, volunteering with a number of adoption support groups and sitting on two local authority adoption panels.

A keen rugby player and supporter, he continues to coach youth players.

The fee for this book is being donated by the author to Behrhorst Partners for Development, a project on partnering with rural Guatemalans to improve health and wellbeing.

Dedicated to mi familia

The Our Story series

This book is part of BAAF's Our Story series, which explores adoption experiences as told by adoptive parents.

Also available in the series:
- *An Adoption Diary* by Maria James
- *Flying Solo* by Julia Wise
- *In Black and White* by Nathalie Seymour
- *A Family Business* by Robert Marsden
- *Together in Time* by Ruth and Ed Royce
- *Adoption Undone* by Karen Carr
- *Take Two* by Laurel Ashton
- *Holding on and Hanging in* by Lorna Miles
- *Dale's Tale* by Helen Jayne
- *Frozen* by Mike Butcher
- *When Daisy met Tommy* by Jules Belle
- *Is it True you have Two Mums?* by Ruby Clay
- *As if I were a Real Boy* by Jeannie and Gordon Mackenzie
- *Becoming Dads* by Pablo Fernández

The series editor

Hedi Argent is an independent family placement consultant, trainer and freelance writer. She is the author of *Find me a Family* (Souvenir Press, 1984), *Whatever Happened to Adam?* (BAAF, 1998), *Related by Adoption* (BAAF, 2004), *One of the Family* (BAAF, 2005), *Ten Top Tips for Placing Children in Families* (BAAF, 2006), *Josh and Jaz have Three Mums* (BAAF, 2007), *Ten Top Tips for Placing Siblings* (BAAF, 2008), and *Ten Top Tips for Supporting Kinship Placements* (BAAF, 2009). She is the co-author of *Taking Extra Care* (BAAF, 1997, with Ailee Kerrane) and *Dealing with Disruption* (BAAF, 2006, with Jeffrey Coleman), and the editor of *Keeping the Doors Open* (BAAF, 1988), *See You Soon* (BAAF, 1995), *Staying Connected* (BAAF, 2002), and *Models of Adoption Support* (BAAF, 2003). She has also written seven illustrated booklets in the children's series published by BAAF.

Introduction

Our children have always loved listening to folk tales from Central America. One of their favourites, which we have in various versions, is the story of the beginning of the world – how men and women and animals were formed. Part of that story tells how the world gained colours, from which the title of this story has been taken.

It is said that the gods were quarrelling (as they always did) because the world was very boring with only black and white to paint it, and gray mixes to paint the dusk and dawn so that the black of the night and the white of the day did not bump into each other too hard. Finally the gods agreed to make some more colours.

One of the gods was walking along and thinking so deeply that he wasn't looking where he was going. He tripped up and hit his head and started to bleed. The god (who like so many of the gods was a bit of a drama queen) squeaked and screamed until he noted that the blood was a different colour, at which point he ran to the other gods and showed them this new colour. They called it red – the third colour to be born.

Another god looked for a colour to paint the feeling of hope – it took him a while but he found it in the shoots of a young plant and showed it to the other gods and they named it green, the fourth colour.

Another one began to look for the heart of the earth and started digging, flinging earth all over the place. When he found it he showed it to the other gods and they called it brown, the fifth colour.

Another god went straight upwards: 'I want to see what colour the world and the sky is.' When he got high enough to see them clearly, he did not know how to bring the colour back down, so he sat and stared until the colour of the world and the sky stuck to his eyes and he went blind. He carefully and painfully climbed down and went to the other gods and said I have the colour of the world and the sky in my eyes – and that was the sixth colour, blue.

Another god was out looking for colours when he heard a child laughing – so when the child wasn't looking he snatched the laugh – leaving the child in tears, which is why children can be laughing one minute and crying the next. The god took the stolen laugh and showed it to the others and they called this, the seventh colour, yellow.

By now the gods were worn out so they had a few drinks and went to sleep. They put all the colours in a box under the ceiba, a huge umbrella tree, but they had not closed it properly and the colours escaped and started to play happily and more and more colours were made. The ceiba tree looked on in wonder and covered the colours to make sure the rain could not wash them away. When the gods woke up they saw all the colours and said to the ceiba tree you have saved the colours – from the top of your head we will paint the world and you will take care of it. So they did and they did not care where the colours landed and the colours splashed on men and women – and that is why there are people of different colours in the world. And to make sure they could keep the colours safe they took the colours and poured them on the macaw – which is why it is so proud of having the brightest colours in the world.

One of our children's favourite versions of this story was written by Subcomandante Marcos, a guerrillero, sometimes described as the post-modern Che Guevara, a leader of the Zapatista Army of the National Liberation who help Mayan farmers in Mexico fight for better treatment for indigenous people. It seems entirely appropriate because in Central America politics, militarism, indigenous rights, myths and children's stories are all jumbled together – in truth it is a true microcosm of reality.

What follows is the story of our family's experiences: adopting two children from Guatemala who will live and grow up in west London, revisiting Guatemala and having contact with the children's birth families and foster family.

PART 1

Red: the colour of death and rebirth

The hallway is full of suitcases and bags. Shoes litter the floor and coats are strewn around. In the kitchen the kettle is gurgling away ready to make that most vital potion – the first cup of proper English tea after you come home. And it is home to all of us even though our backgrounds are wide and varied and we have arrived here by what might be described as not the most straightforward of means. We are just back from a trip to our children's birthplace, Guatemala, and my mind goes back to our first visit in 1996.

Elly and I were not married then but were already firmly committed to intercountry adoption. We had been together for a long time and had had more than enough attempts at IVF of all varieties. We had looked into domestic adoption but had been given short shrift – we simply were not needed by a system where exact ethnic matching was seen to take precedence over finding families for children. We felt that the decision had been made in a formulaic manner without actually looking into our backgrounds and capabilities and communicated to us extremely poorly (actually quite rudely). But we were not to be deterred – we wanted to be a family and we wanted to be able to give a family and home to a child or children who needed one.

So in 1995 we approached our local authority to ask for an intercountry adoption home study. The local authority had subcontracted intercountry adoption home studies to an agency in south-west London and we were put in touch with them.

The first requirement was to go on a three-day preparation course – well, two evenings and a very short day. Frankly, the content was poor. The attendees included social workers, teachers, lawyers, other professionals, "mixed race" couples, people who had lived and worked overseas, and all of them had done their homework before they started. More importantly, the course leaders did not have a visceral understanding of what being part of a transracial adoptive family means, and no way of helping us to become truly prepared for the journey facing us. They gave sparse information on various aspects of the UK system and even less on the sending countries. They showed some very outdated videos with doubtful relevance. They offered very little insight into the feelings and developmental outcomes of transracial adoptees. They did not even give us a reading list.

The course, which incidentally was by no means cheap, left us upset and frustrated. We knew the UK system was not set up to help intercountry adoption: there was an undercurrent of antagonism and opposition, there was no real official information and it seemed the whole idea was to put as many obstacles in our way as possible, in the hope that we would give up and go away.

Luckily we and other attendees had become members of various intercountry adoption support groups: Overseas Adoption Support and Information Service (OASIS),

Association of Families Adopting from Abroad (AFAA) and in our case the Guatemalan Families Association (GFA).

We had already started to read and share information from some of the books that had been recommended by other adopters. We met, via the GFA, families who had already adopted from Guatemala and their wonderful, beautiful children.

There were a number of things that made us look to Guatemala as our country of choice. It was an established route and one where we felt we would not be trailblazing (my respect and admiration go out to all those who have fulfilled this role and continue to do so). The children were in foster care and not in institutions, which would increase the child's chances of making healthy attachments. In addition, and for us most importantly, the children were not abandoned without links to their birth families and histories, but were relinquished, which meant that the birth mothers played an important part in the process, coming to sign papers on a number of occasions, being interviewed by UK consular staff and undergoing DNA testing to prove their relationship with the child. Finally, we thought we would genuinely be able to commit to supporting the language and culture.

All this was great in theory but we felt we needed to confirm our choice of Guatemala as the country we wanted to adopt from so we arranged to go on holiday there. We were also able to meet with old friends of Elly's in Belize. It was a fantastic journey. We went to places and travelled in ways we knew we would not be able to once we had children with us. We took the chicken buses (converted US school buses painted in amazing brightly coloured liveries) everywhere, mingling with the people, walking round Lake Atitlan on the small footpaths and eating at the roadside *comedores* ("restaurants" where you ate what the family was eating). We encountered for the first time the incredible generosity of spirit of the

3

Guatemalan people. We also saw the contrast between the gentle nature, hospitality, creativity, and the sense of community and beauty of so many of the people, and the legacy of more than 30 years of civil war, with its consequent lack of trust in authority, absence of even the most basic support facilities and the depths to which members of those same communities had sunk.

We crossed the border to Belize where we had to walk through the border zone and change buses because of the ongoing enmity between the two countries. We drove around Belize with our friends, stayed a few nights on a tiny caye (pronounced key), a sand spit of an island no more than 500 metres by 250 and with a maximum height of about two metres: battery-powered electricity, crude wooden huts but roosting ospreys overhead, where the hammocks swung between the palm trees.

But in Guatemala especially we also came face to face with the extreme poverty which wracked the country and the towns, with bodies of old and young lying by the roadside, with stories of babies being abandoned near the fire stations – the firemen also run all paramedic services – and being left exposed in the forests and jungle. We could see the need for support for the communities but we could also appreciate that for some children this would not happen fast enough to save them and that alternative ways of finding them a family was a viable and ethical choice.

So we found it really easy to commit ourselves to Guatemala and its people – and it is a commitment that we have never questioned or regretted and which we embrace even more as time goes by and our knowledge and links grow stronger and wider.

Guatemala – some background information

Guatemala has been described as the most beautiful place in the world. It is a country that has amazing natural beauty – lakes surrounded by mountains and

4

volcanoes, jungles and forests which have swallowed Mayan ruins, orchids and exotic birds, jaguars and turtles on the Caribbean beaches. But this beauty masks its bloody and tortuous past.

Guatemala has the highest proportion of indigenous peoples in Central and Latin America. Catholic and Evangelical churches have roughly equal numbers of members – but all the while traditional Mayan religions and spirituality continues. A tiny minority hold the power and the wealth. Millions of Guatemalans work (often illegally) in the US.

Illiteracy, infant mortality, stunting and malnutrition are amongst the worst in the region and in some cases in the world. Life expectancy is one of the lowest. Huge areas are plagued by drug traffickers, organised crime and *maras* – violent street gangs many of whom have been extradited from the US.

All this has been exacerbated by the events of 1954 when the democratic government of Guatemala was overthrown by an army coup orchestrated and paid for by the CIA (whose Director's brother was the head of the United Fruit Company, later Chiquita, which opposed the land reforms being proposed by the then government because they threatened the company's interests). This coup led to a series of further internecine struggles in the army, a growing anti-communist paranoia and state-sponsored terrorism of the indigenous and the poor – culminating in a 30-year civil war that only came to an end in 1996.

According to the UN-sponsored Commission for Historical Clarification, government forces and state-sponsored paramilitaries were found to be responsible for 93 per cent of the human rights violations recorded during the civil war. These included the murder of over 200,000 people, mostly Mayan and other civilians, the destruction of more than 450 villages or communities, and the displacement of over one million people (many of whose deaths in the jungles and mountains or over the borders in other states were never recorded).

And yet this is also the heartland of the Mayan people – one of the world's great civilisations. At its height, between 250 and 900 AD, the Mayan civilization built hundreds of cities across Central America with the largest concentration of independent city states in the Peten region; many of the ruins can still be seen today whilst others continue to be discovered under the cover of the jungle that has overwhelmed them. These cities had incredibly well developed structures and systems, and their advances in mathematics and astronomy were far ahead of their Western equivalents.

After 900 AD the Maya abandoned many of their cities, especially in the lowlands, as thousands of the people were killed off by drought-induced famines. The remaining cities gathered into regional kingdoms, which preserved many of the aspects of Mayan culture, but none of them equalled the power or size of the Classic period.

In 1519 the first of the Spanish expeditions to Guatemala arrived led by Pedro de Alvarado – and was accompanied by the first of many epidemics that were to devastate the native population. Guatemala did not have the mineral wealth of Mexico and Peru so was not considered important. A number of capitals built by the Spaniards were destroyed by earthquakes – the penultimate of which is Antigua, now a UNESCO World Heritage site. Guatemala's main products were sugarcane, cocoa, blue anil dye, red cochineal and precious woods used in artwork throughout the Spanish empire.

Between 1821 and 1871 Guatemala and many of its neighbours fought (often against each other) to gain independence from the Spanish Empire, the Mexican

Empire and the United Provinces of Central America. Guatemala's "Liberal Revolution" came in 1871 under the leadership of Justo Rufino Barrios, who worked hard to modernise the country. Coffee was introduced in this period. Unfortunately, Barrios also had ambitions over his neighbours and was killed in 1885 in battle in El Salvador.

From 1898 to 1920 the dictator Manuel Estrada Cabrera ruled over Guatemala. He became dictator with the support of the United Fruit Company, which gained a position of influence and power that was to be hugely detrimental over the coming decades.

After the Second World War a military junta called Guatemala's first free election, won by Juan Jose Arevalo Bermejo. His policies were based on the "US New Deal" and were called "Christian Socialism" but were reviled by the upper classes, landowners and big business as "communist", thus causing irrational fears in the US.

When Arevalo's successor, Jacobo Arbenz, also freely elected and a socialist, started to bring in land reforms designed to rid his country of some of the iniquities left over from colonial times, he was overthrown by the coup paid for and led by the CIA in 1954 (with considerable support from the United Fruit Company).

From this time until the end of the civil war in 1996 there followed a series of military dictators with the brief intermission of the Mendez Montenegro government, which saw the spawning of many of the secret rightist paramilitary organisations that developed into the infamous death squads. The US government continued to support the Guatemalan army with training, weapons and money. The US used Guatemala as a base from which to train anti-Castro Cubans, built airstrips to support the Bay of Pigs invasion and supplied Special Forces to train the army, until in 1979, US President Jimmy Carter banned all military aid to Guatemala because of "the widespread and systematic abuse of human rights". Unfortunately this was already too late and successive military governments continued their campaigns to suppress all opposition, by using torture, forced disappearances and scorched earth policies.

In addition, in 1976 the country had been struck by a major earthquake which destroyed several cities and caused more than 25,000 recorded deaths.

Another notable event occurred in 1980, when a group of indigenous people took over the Spanish Embassy in protest. The Government's response was to launch an assault that led to a fire and killed almost everyone inside – which the Government then blamed on the protestors, a claim disputed by the Spanish Ambassador himself, who said that the police had set fires deliberately in order to cover up the fact that they had killed most of the people inside the Embassy. One of those killed was the father of Rigoberta Menchu, who subsequently won the Nobel Peace prize in 1992 for her efforts to publicise the government-sponsored genocide of the indigenous people of Guatemala.

After the 1996 peace accord the UN-sponsored Commission for Historical Clarification set to work trying to make sense of all the claims and counter-claims and attempts to evade responsibility. It found that Maya Native Americans made up 83 per cent of the victims and that 93 per cent of the atrocities had been carried out by government armed forces. Fundamental to the work of the UN Commission was the work of the National Reconciliation Commission, which wrote and presented a report, *Guatemala: Nunca mas* (Guatemala: Never again), on 24 April 1998. Two days later one of its authors and main advocates, Bishop Gerardi, was beaten to death with a concrete slab. Three years later in 2001 three army officers were convicted of his murder.

In 1999 President Bill Clinton apologised for the US support of military forces and intelligence units, which had engaged in violent and widespread repression.

Unfortunately, implementation of the peace accords has never really gained any momentum – some say that things are now going backwards. The UN states that the indigenous people are still marginalised by discrimination and violence. The UN Human Development Index still shows that in terms of life expectancy, income, school enrolment and access to medicine, Guatemala ranks the lowest of any North, Central or South American country other than Haiti.

So back in England we waited for a social worker to be allocated for our home study.

The agency delayed and delayed even though they had banked our cheque for the thousands of pounds of fees they were charging. We kept calling and writing to keep the pressure on and in the end a social worker was appointed – and this time luck was very definitely in our favour. She was independent, having retired some while before to be a writer, and was an adoptive parent herself: hers were transracial domestic adoptions from the days before this was effectively "banned". What an inspiration and font of knowledge she became. She truly fulfilled the preparation requirement of the home study. Our sessions were serious and intense, and actually really enjoyable and, more importantly, continued to open our eyes to adoption and all the issues associated with it.

Both Elly and I had spent a lot of time overseas and working with children. Elly had worked as a teacher in Nigeria. Her sister lives in Japan and has six children, all of whom Elly helped care for during their first months. She is both a Special Needs and English as a Second Language (ESL) teacher so has loads of experience working with children for whom English is not the first language and who, for whatever reason, have various difficulties with academic learning.

I had worked with institutionalised children in Italy and, while living in Japan, had become an unofficial carer for Elly's nephews and niece, spending many happy hours looking after any number of them as well as the neighbours' children. I had also been privileged to care for my sisters' two children on occasion. We were therefore able to have some really in-depth discussions about racism and how it affects individuals and society.

Our social worker, having questioned our motivation and capacities, suggested to us that we consider being approved for two children straight away rather than sequentially as we had envisaged, since she felt it would be better for the children coming from such a different environment to have each other as support. We took a bit of time to think about that idea – would we be good enough – could we cope – was it right for the children – and came to the conclusion that it seemed like a very positive course and so we agreed and committed to it wholeheartedly.

Eventually the time came for us to sign our agreement to the report written about us. Our social worker had managed to turn the bland and formulaic official questions into something that told our stories and made us sound like real people. Our reasons for wanting to adopt, our support networks, our reading and learning all came over as a coherent whole. We signed and waited for the home study to be attached to our referees' statements and to be submitted to our agency's adoption panel.

Unfortunately, there was a problem. Our social worker had produced it in one word processing programme, the agency used another. So rather than converting it they chose to retype it – and then the typist went off sick for a few weeks! We offered to get it converted for them but they refused; it took a few months before we finally had a panel date.

Meanwhile, we had also got married to ensure that we qualified as a couple. It was a smallish affair and the ceremony was kept as short as possible – as were the speeches. In fact the best man's speech was just 'Ladies and Gentlemen, Stevan and Elly'. Afterwards we went for a meal and finished up at Ronnie Scott's for a fantastic night of salsa and jazz.

At that time it was considered inappropriate for prospective adopters to attend panel, so we waited at home, available should our social worker wish to ask any supplementary questions, while our fates were being decided.

After what seemed like hours the call finally came through – we had passed panel and subject to the agency decision maker approving the recommendation, we were approved intercountry adopters. To say that this was a relief is an understatement. We were bouncing off the ceiling – effectively this meant we were going to become parents – whose parents was up to fate, but nevertheless it looked like it was going to happen, and all the losses and failures of "natural" methods and IVF were finally behind us.

The agency decision maker agreed (more celebrations but also a renewed sense of urgency – we wanted things to happen and now) and our papers were sent to the Department of Health (DoH), the UK government department then responsible for intercountry adoption. As they say in the Army, "hurry up and wait" – this seemed to be the way things worked in intercountry adoption: bursts of intense activity and pressure followed by periods of frustrating impotence and incompetence. Despite frequent calls, faxes and fees paid, we fumed while very little happened for quite a few weeks.

Eventually we were told that our certificate of eligibility to adopt was ready and we needed to get our papers notarised, legalised and authenticated prior to returning them to the DoH for onward transmission via the Foreign and Commonwealth Office (FCO) to the embassy in Guatemala City to be collected by our agency's legal representative!

We arranged for our dossier to be sent to a notary and for the witnesses and referees to meet us there. We all signed our various bits and pieces, and then everything was notarised; using a cunning form of words our notary fulfilled all the differing requirements.

I then took the dossier to the FCO where (having paid the fee) they were able to legalise the documents and verify that the signature and stamps matched those on their records.

Off again to the Guatemalan Embassy. Dropped the dossier off, paid fee and was told to collect the dossier next morning with the FCO's stamps authenticated as genuine. Had a great chat with the embassy staff – their friendliness and support have remained a very positive influence ever since.

Next day I collected the dossier and sent it overnight to the DoH for onward transmission to the British Embassy in Guatemala City. It had taken less than 48 hours for us to do our bit of the process. It then took the DoH more than a month to photocopy the file and get it into the diplomatic bag. Finally the news came through – our papers were in Guatemala and the next crucial phase could commence on our journey to become a family.

In the absence of any UK intercountry adoption agencies at the time, we had decided to go with a US agency to help facilitate our adoption in Guatemala. This agency had negotiated a number of successful overseas adoptions in the UK and we felt quite content that they were also ethical and efficient.

We had been assigned a lawyer in Guatemala, Guillermo, and he went to pick up the papers from the British Embassy, after all sorts of delays and unnecessary hassles. The papers were then authenticated once more by the Guatemalan Foreign Embassy and we were ready for a referral.

A few weeks pass... No news.

Then suddenly just before midnight a phone call from the head of our agency in the US... they have a possible match... a boy of about two and a little girl of eight weeks in the same foster home. Are we interested?

As I type this my eyes mist up and my hands shake with the remembered strength of the feelings. We look at each other on the two telephone extensions and one of us manages to blurt out 'yes of course' (I still have no idea which of us spoke or if it was both of us in communion). A few minutes later the fax whirls and two completely blurred photos come out accompanied by one page of medical reports and basic details.

So this is to be our family!!

Two fuzzy pictures, one called Veronica and the other called Roger. Veronica is very badly malnourished and has all of the physical symptoms that accompany the condition. Roger seems to be OK. We bounce around the house hugging and crying and laughing and completely overwhelmed with the emotions that have been building up to this point. It is too late to tell anyone – we so want to share our joy but cannot until the morning.

To be truthful I have no idea how we made it through that night – were we prosaic and just shuffled off to bed – did we have a wee dram or two (Elly being a true Scot) – or anything else? No idea. Next day we started to share our news with family and friends, cautiously saying nothing was sure yet but we hoped that we might be making progress. Our friends, made through intercountry adoption groups, truly understood and laughed and cried with us, sharing our release of pent up emotion.

A few days later we get photos in the post. We are no longer reliant on black splodges but have a few colour images, not brilliant, but so fantastic for us to see. Elly immediately names Veronica lemon squidge – she is all wrapped up in a yellow blanket and her face is all pinky brown and well … squidgy. Roger is serious and handsome and looks like the villain from the second Crocodile Dundee film, Hechter Ubarry.

Each photo is examined in exquisite detail. Most would say you cannot get attached to a photo, but you can. You can start to invest hopes and dreams and joy in these images.

Over the next few weeks and months we get more information, medical reports, paperwork going into the court system and being rejected or accepted by the Guatemalan system working in its own inimitable way.

Then comes a body blow but the news is both good and bad. Roger's birth mother has asked for him back and, of course, the lawyer has immediately returned him to her care and undone all the legal paperwork, which had given him custody. This is good news intellectually because it shows that the Guatemalan system does function correctly, and birth mothers have the right to change their minds, and that this is respected even if the lawyers have made significant financial investments.

It is bad news emotionally because we are back to stage one, and we mourn our loss. But we knew this was a possibility so we regroup and prepare to move on. A few days later the agency and Guillermo talk to us about another little boy in the same foster home as Veronica, a little bit older but with an established relationship with her – what the US would call a "social sibling". His name is Osvaldo and we are sent photos.

I don't have words to describe the feelings when I saw Ossie, as he was quickly nicknamed. Some chord in my heart was struck quietly and decisively. Again as I sit here writing this, huge waves of feelings swell up and overwhelm me. This adoption lark is not easy on the soul.

Of course we accept the referral. But now we encounter a major obstacle. Because we have, for perfectly proper reasons, had to change our referral, the UK is now objecting to our accepting social siblings, which they hadn't, illogically, when dealing with Roger and Veronica. Latterly the regulations and then the law have been changed to exclude social siblings, but at the time the law and regulations were silent in this regard. We look around for any UK research to shine a light on this matter, and Prof. Peter Selman (to whom we are and always will be profoundly grateful for his kindness and generosity of spirit) points us to a one liner in Prof. Michael Rutter's work on Romanian orphans, which says, and I paraphrase freely, there is no reason not to accept social siblings where there is a genuine relationship and the age is not too close.

So off we go and ask our agency to get a social worker in Guatemala to write a report outlining the quality of the relationship between Ossie and Veronica, who by now have spent six months or more together in foster care. The former head of the social workers' professional body in Guatemala, who has social work qualifications from the US as well as Guatemala, writes the report and it is favourable. We send it to the DoH and wait. Nothing happens. Without their acceptance of the match we cannot proceed in Guatemala. We try to find out what is happening – no one will talk to us or reply to our urgent letters and faxes.

In the meantime, Hurricane Mitch has struck Guatemala leaving behind it a trail of destruction and disaster. This further complicates matters because communications, always fragile at best, are pretty much destroyed. We lose track of Ossie's birth family and it takes quite a while for the workers to re-establish contact. We just keep hoping they are OK – thousands have been killed and/or are missing. Eventually word comes through that they are OK but have lost even the little they had.

A friend, who is a social worker, tells us we have the right to see our dossier in the DoH. So we invoke the right with all the necessary references to regulations. We are given a date to come to the department

We think we are going to see our paperwork, instead we are both shocked and distressed to be confronted by about a dozen people sitting around a table facing us, including the head of social policy, our area social work inspector, the adoption section manager and a senior civil servant. They do not clarify their agenda for the meeting but it becomes clear that most of them are hostile – some in principle because they object to intercountry adoption, some object to transracial adoption, some object to social siblings, some object to anything that the US adoption system supports. Apparently, we are expected to persuade them of our case to adopt Veronica and Osvaldo. We were neither expecting nor warned of such a confrontation.

We fight our corner as best we can. We try to marshal our arguments as we speak, but we have not prepared ourselves for this onslaught. We try to scrabble together coherent thoughts and the right vocabulary on the fly. We are shocked when we are told that our agency should not have made our social worker change her recommendation from "two children" to "twins or a sibling group". Precedent is blandly dismissed as a mistake if it goes against the personal views of the people sitting opposite. The well written and well prepared report written by an experienced professional is dismissed – too American influenced and too much on our side!

We never get to see our dossier. We leave in despair. That night we talk and talk trying to find a way through this seeming impasse. This is the letter we write to the adoption section manager in the early hours of the next morning:

Adoption Section
Department of Health

21 September 1998

Dear _____,

Re: The adoption of Osvaldo Hernan Suchite Gonzales and Veronica Maybeli Felipe

Thank you for meeting us today, we are appreciative that you all gave up so much of your own time.

However, we felt that we should write to you to voice our disquiet after the meeting.

At the start of the meeting you asked us why we were there and we explained that we had asked for the opportunity to view our file. We felt there had been significant delays in processing what we perceived to be a simple administrative task – sending our second home study to our notary and then on to the Foreign Office etc. No one explained the purpose you had for the meeting. We had not been informed of your agenda or the number of people who were to be present.

Thus we felt unable to argue our case adequately since we had not had a chance to prepare ourselves or enlist professional counsel, and not being social work professionals we both felt that we were at a distinct disadvantage and vulnerable. We therefore found the interviewer's remark that she had "not been persuaded by our arguments" at the end of the meeting to be very distressing. It reinforced our impression that we had been attempting, unwittingly, to defend our position in a tribunal situation.

We had no reason to believe that your department was reviewing our case and I am sure you can sympathise with the shock caused when this came out during the course of the meeting. We were unaware that you considered that we were setting a precedent, and that the decision in the "O" case had been a mistake. Our distress was compounded when we were told that our agency was wrong to instruct our social worker not to put us forward for the adoption of two children but for a sibling group.

We were gratified that you agreed that errors such as these had been made at all levels in the UK, which had exacerbated the situation. Nevertheless we left the meeting without any satisfactory explanation for the causes of the delay in sending out our duplicate home study. Merely to cite "holidays" as a reason is wholly inadequate. We have still not been afforded the opportunity to view our file.

We feel we have been the victims of mismanagement, the cultural gap between the UK, the US and Guatemala and communications failures.

We feel that today we and our children may have been "failed" by your department when we didn't even know we were sitting a test. We hope that sufficient evidence will be presented to satisfy you that Veronica and Osvaldo have a relationship that falls within the parameters of your definition of social siblings. We remain committed to the adoption of Veronica and Osvaldo and earnestly hope that they should not be made to suffer further by being parted permanently.

We would appreciate a copy of the minutes of the meeting for comment as soon as they are available.

Yours sincerely
Stevan Whitehead and Elly Young

We then sit back and wait for a response. It has become clear to the DoH that we are not going to give up on "our children", as we already thought of them. We make it clear that we will take as many measures as we need to, involve the DoH in as many legal and professional confrontations as necessary and incur as much expense as it will take. So they start to look for a fudge and find one by saying that if our local authority is prepared to accept the match they will drop their objections. Luckily, our local authority takes the hint and does.

Even so, the DoH drops a spanner in the works. Because the children are not related they both have their individual files in the Guatemalan courts. Thus they both need to have their own original version of our certificate of eligibility to adopt. It is acceptable to have a photocopy with an original signature attached, but the DoH argues that if we have two certificates with signatures, and that both say we are entitled to adopt two children, then in fact we could adopt four, which we are not entitled to do. We ask, could we have two certificates saying one child, and they say 'no' because we then could not adopt two children! We ask, could we have one saying we are entitled to adopt these two named children and a copy with an original signature, but they say 'no that is not how we do things'. A month is wasted in futile discussions and requests while the children get older, as do we, and our nerves are fraying and our tempers are getting very short.

Then the paediatrician, who has been looking after the children, raises some significant concerns about Veronica's development. She is nowhere near starting to walk, her co-ordination is poor and her head circumference is below the norm. The word microcephalic is mentioned, so immediately Elly goes off and finds the microcephaly support group and gets loads of information about likely prognosis and outcomes. We never questioned whether she would be ours – just what work we might need to do to care for her fully and ensure she reaches her potential. Dr Montiel, the paediatrician, arranges for her to get some physiotherapy and the difference is visible really quickly in the photographs. She is still delayed, but the thought is now that it is more likely to be related to her significant malnutrition in utero and during her first weeks of life.

A UK couple, great friends of ours, adopting twins just a month or so younger than Veronica, are going out to Guatemala for the twins' first birthday. Since Dr S, the adoptive father, is a GP, they are allowed to meet our two in Dr Montiel's consulting rooms. They make a video and Dr S has a chance to consult with Dr Montiel about Veronica and Ossie's progress. Ossie is shy and does not seem to have a lot of vocabulary for a two-year-old but physically he is robust and once he gets used to the situation he smiles and relates well to his foster carer. So we are a bit reassured but we still have not found a way round the impasses at the DoH.

Finally, Guillermo just gets on with it – ignoring protocol he uses our original Certificate of Eligibility to Adopt on Veronica's dossier in the Guatemalan courts and gets her adoption finalised. He then makes a notarised copy, leaves it on her file, takes the original and starts Ossie off through the system. I wish I could say that the completion of Veronica's adoption is joy unbounded. Of course we are overjoyed that she is now definitely our daughter, but we are again faced with a terrible quandary. Of course we want to go and bring Veronica home as soon as possible but in doing so we will separate her from Ossie

– in fact we will swan into his life as his future parents, grab his sister and swan off again. What damage will that do to him? How will he see us when we come back? We cannot see any solution other than just hoping for the best and taking as many things to help him through the wait as we can.

First trip to Guatemala

So we make plans to go out to Guatemala as soon as possible. We book the flights, two out ... three back. How exciting is that! We book into the Marriott as requested by our agency since they are very used to adoptive families, have all the facilities and necessary security, and a famous buffet breakfast!

Because we know that it is important to make Veronica's transition a smooth one, and that we need to help Ossie to understand that we are coming back for him, we are aware we need to stage the introductions and transfer especially carefully. It has been agreed to set up introductions so that the foster mother and her family can show that we are their friends and that it is safe to stay with us. So a series of increasingly longer visits has been planned, culminating in overnights with us in the hotel.

Finally, the time comes to fly out – bags packed, courage tightened to the sticking point, holding hands we venture out together. The flight is uneventful or we are so numb we don't notice a thing. Not sure which.

The hotel bus is there to collect us and off we go to the Marriott. We check in, go upstairs, unpack, especially all the children's clothes and toys we have brought for our two, and also for the other children in the foster home, get showered and sit and wait. Guillermo is due in an hour or so and we want to look our best. Another friend from the UK who is in Guatemala City comes up to see us (and distract us thankfully) and offers to take videos and photos. Finally the call comes from reception and we go down in the lift.

The lift doors open and there sitting on the big leather sofas are a group of smiling people – Guillermo, his wife and two daughters, Silvia the foster mother, her brother who has driven them down and, of course, Veronica and Osvaldo. I look at Ossie and he just sticks his arms up and we cuddle for the first time, so naturally and so deeply I cannot explain it, other than that somehow we were fated to meet.

Meanwhile Veronica and Elly are getting to know each other and in the midst of all of this we are embracing all the adults and saying broken 'hellos' and 'thank yous' and 'so fantastic to meet you finally'.

Then we all get back in the lift and pile into our room. It is now quite crowded with bodies on the beds, sitting on the chairs and the floor. All of the clothes and toys are being scattered about, played with, commented on, and Ossie and Veronica are smiling, looking to Silvia for reassurance, obviously well aware and used to Guillermo and his wife. Eventually Guillermo and family go, as does Silvia's brother and our UK friend and we are left, just the five of us: Silvia and our "family of four".

Everything calms down. We begin getting to know each other a lot better. Silvia starts our childcare 101 class, showing how she changes their nappies, gets them dressed and undressed; there are some unfamiliar extra body wraps which are "a must" in Central America. The kids are getting tired so lie down for a nap on one of the beds. We sit in silence just admiring them – they are so beautiful; they have the most amazing temperaments, quietly coping with the chaos around them and the unfamiliar surroundings.

Eventually it is time for Silvia, Ossie and Veronica to go back with Guillermo and his wife and we sit back and reflect on what was one of the most amazing days of our lives. All of our fears about the children not liking us are long gone. They seem to know who we are and they seem to be accepting us as friends of Silvia, and thus OK people. Our hopes that the transition will not be too bad seem to be growing on firm ground. We eat in the hotel and collapse into bed exhausted but happy. But before we go off, we write a quick email (yes, we had entered the modern age) to all our friends and family.

Dear friends

Well, here we are in Guatemala having met the two most beautiful kids in the world – and that is now official and irrefutable – we know, we were here!

We waited until just after 5pm this evening to meet them and Silvia, their foster mother, and Guillermo and Diana, our lawyer and his wife. As you can imagine we were just a little anxious prior to their arrival, but successfully managed to fill the day with hanging around the pool and going shopping! A long time friend from Acton who has been out here two weeks or so, was with us as her little boy was coming too, because he shares our foster mother and our lawyer. When the moment finally arrived, after a bit of a false start due to a minor communication problem, we got the phone call to say they were in the lobby and we went off to the lift with our hearts in our mouths. The lift doors opened as we got to the ground floor and there waiting were Veronica and Osvaldo and the rest of the party.

To say we were overwhelmed by the moment is an understatement, but being very British we kept a stiff upper lip or two and greeted all the adults and got to work getting to know our kids. We all went back up to our room – a little cramped but at least it gave us some privacy – and got out a few toys and offered coffee, juice and biscuits all round. We then got down to the serious stuff of playing on the floor with some of the presents we had brought.

I am sure some of you have heard Elly talking about how I fell in love with Osvaldo the very second I saw his photo for the first time, and have always felt a special bond with our little boy. Well, real life is even better and hundreds of times stronger. From the first time I picked him up it felt as if we had always been together – I have no idea how we will cope with being apart until he comes home. Meanwhile Elly and Veronica were hard at it getting to know each other – and it appeared to be pretty much instantaneous as well. Obviously it helped that Silvia and Guillermo and Diana were all around but it really did seem ordained. Veronica is a much more reserved child than Ossie but Elly soon had her laughing and playing games. We were delighted to see Osvaldo playing with Veronica and pushing cars to her and she would gamely (if a trifle crudely) throw them back in his general direction, give or take 180 degrees. Our friend was valiantly manning the video for the first hour, so we have a true Cecil B De Mille extravaganza of our first meeting.

Guillermo and Diana went off to take one of their daughters – they have eight children – to the University, where she has an entrance exam tomorrow. We carried on playing with the children and trying to establish a rapport with Silvia, which in truth was very easy as she is a really lovely person and the kids adore her.

Veronica by now had really mellowed into the situation, assisted by the fact that Ossie had fallen asleep and was snoring quietly on one of the beds. She was now the star of the show and receiving the undivided attention of *four adults – and playing to the crowd unashamedly. She walked – well, OK, she staggered like a very well oiled sailor – from Elly to Silvia to me, laughing and smiling all the time. She spent at least half an hour looking at some of the photos we had brought for Ossie to keep. She was particularly fascinated by her cousin Elena, into whom she assiduously rubbed half-eaten biscuits. She made a toy out of a piece of hotel notepaper, playing peekaboo, blowing kisses to it and with it, and making hats.*

Finally, Guillermo and Diana came back with their daughter and took the children away to sleep and dream happy dreams and come back tomorrow.

We went off to a tearful supper, with all of the pent up emotions finally coming out, and now just six hours after they arrived and three hours after they left, here we are celebrating and sharing our happiness with our friends.

Have we got any doubts or regrets? None. We are a family at last and forever and words cannot describe how good that feels.

Stevan and Elly
Hotel Marriott El Dorado
Guatemala City

The next day Silvia comes with the children and we go off on a trip to the zoo. The children are ecstatic – they have obviously been before and know their favourite animals. Ossie loves playing hide and seek around the Mayan stelae (monuments), which are grouped around the open areas. Veronica loves sitting in the stroller we have brought – a luxury she is not used to. We stop for lunch at the café by

25

the entrance and Ossie demonstrates an impressive ability to eat huge quantities and drink directly from the litre bottles of water (this is something he will never lose).

We get a chance to meet Dr Montiel – it turns out he did his PhD in Liverpool and is still a fan of Liverpool Football Club and the Beatles. He gives us a more extensive review of Veronica and Ossie's medical backgrounds and hands us Veronica's medical records including all of her immunisations.

We go back to the hotel and meet Guillermo and go off to get Veronica's passport photos. She has to have her hair slicked back with water, something she lets us know very quickly she does not appreciate by howling long and loud – good lungs! And one ear must be showing. Eventually the photos are taken and are deemed acceptable so off we go to the passport office. There are huge queues of people – but there are also "agents" who, for a fee, get you around the back door and straight to their favoured officers. An hour or two later we are clutching Veronica's passport.

We have missed her birth mother interview at the British Embassy (it happened before we arrived) but have been told everything went OK so we make our appointment to get our entry clearance for Veronica. We also tell the consul that we would like to sign the papers to confirm that Elly has met Osvaldo and is happy for the adoption to proceed, so that when it is time for him to come home we do not both have to travel. We had heard terrible stories of families returning to bring home a second child where the first child thought they were being taken back to be rejected; or where the parents left the first child with relatives and the child thought the parents were not coming back. So our plan was for one of us (probably me) to travel to bring Ossie home, while Elly waited in the UK with Veronica.

We hand in the passport and are told it will take a couple of days for the requisite stamps. So Guillermo makes plans for the next two days. First we arrange to go to meet Ossie's birth mother and birth family and the *buscadora* (literally, searcher) who introduced both Ossie's and Veronica's families to Guillermo and the adoption system. It is a very long drive. Many of the roads still show the marks of Hurricane Mitch. We pass a Bailey-type bridge, hundreds of tons of steel girders bolted together in the middle of a flood plain. It is explained it has been washed down from about 10 kilometres up river and we pause to think of the awesome power of the wind and water associated with a hurricane. We think about the fear it must imbue in people whose only shelter is houses made of a form of wattle and daub with palm frond roofs. It is easy to understand how their religion is still a mixture of Christian and animist.

We drive on till we get to the town where the *buscadora* Dona Betty lives. She is obviously one of the "great and the good". She is the widow of a former mayor ("disappeared" during the long civil war) and her children run three local "bus" services, she has unofficial foster kids she is educating – a real bustling, strong lady giving as much as she can to her community, who is easily approached by all levels of society. She invites us into her home and gives us a bit of background on the birth families. Then we hop into the car again and go off to see Ossie's grandparents first.

We park at the side of a non-descript part of a small country road – no recognisable community and definitely no services. Dona Betty heads off up over the bank and a few minutes later calls us up. We climb over the bank to see a small hut with an external kitchen space with an open fire between two rocks. A group of adults and children are waiting for us. The older couple look exhausted and the woman obviously has problems moving around. These are the grandparents but they are actually a lot younger than us. The grandmother had dislocated a hip in childbirth some while ago but has never been able to get it fixed. She has had fourteen children and less than half of them have survived. She is still having children and the young ones around her are a mixture of her children and grandchildren. None of the children wear a top *and* a bottom – it seems you get one or the other. It brings reality into focus very abruptly. We promise we will not let Ossie forget where he comes from and we will bring him back as often as we can.

Ossie's mother, as is customary, lives with her new husband's family. So we get back in the car and go off to find them. Again Dona Betty goes off to scout things out and comes back to tell us it is best if we go down the road a bit so as not to bring the family to public attention, which could be dangerous. Ossie's birth mother will be coming back from work soon and she will come down to meet us. Again we wait and wait. Guillermo finds a tortoise, which he puts in the back of the car to take home to his kids. A soldier jogs past keeping fit – he looks impressive. Men ride past on skinny horses, others are pulling carts or swamped with loads of firewood or palm fronds. Eventually a pretty, shy, petite woman can be seen walking down to meet us. This is the woman who is making such a huge sacrifice to change the life of her son and give us the opportunity to care for him and love him. What can we say or do to thank her and reassure her we will do our best for him? Silent tearful hugs follow – there are no words, just touch and looks and silent guarantees. This is some form of primal communication that cannot be explained but somehow works, brings certainty and understanding and trust. Eventually we part and Guillermo finishes some outstanding paperwork, and we watch her walk wearily up the hill. We know we will be back, but what will we find?

A long drive home to the Marriott, sitting silently in the car, all emotions spent. The only noise, the tortoise scrabbling in the cardboard box in the boot.

The next day is a big one – we get Ossie and Veronica all day and overnight!

Again Silvia brings them along and gets us all settled down. She goes through the routine again and explains they are not keen on baths but not to let that put us off. We head off to some safe places we have been told about – tourist markets and museums. On the way home we stop off at a supermarket just outside the hotel to buy some essential supplies and bump into another family with a little Guatemalan girl in a sling. They do not look or sound American and we get into a conversation. It turns out they are Dutch but have lived and worked in the UK. We exchange contact details and hope to meet again.

We come back and order the famous Marriott burgers from room service. We reckon that since they are American size, i.e. huge, we will be able to share one between an adult and a child. So we halve them … wrong!

Ossie demolishes his half and sets off on mine. Luckily the girls' appetites are more dainty and I can gather a few scraps they leave behind.

We run a bath – the kids jump in – they love it. It later transpires that at the foster home there is no hot water. I wouldn't enjoy cold baths either. We get them out and wrap them in the huge white fluffy towels the hotel provides. The contrast with their beautiful brown skin is exquisite but serves as a reminder of what we may have to face – however, at this moment we are just luxuriating in their company and the joy they are bringing us and we hope we are bringing them. The hotel staff (who could not have been more positive about us and adoption and the kids) have set up two cribs in the room so we hug and rock the children until they are ready for bed and then tuck them up. They fall asleep immediately and we soon follow them.

Next morning we wake to the sound of the two of them playing together through the bars of their cots. There is no better way in this world to wake than to the sound of children's happiness. On our way down to the famous breakfast, we look around at the other adoptive families, all

American, some of them exhausted and not having an easy time of it, and thank the stars and fate that we seem to be having such a smooth transition. We go off to the buffet – the staff are obviously used to this – so we carry the children and they load the plates for us and bring them back to our table – and when I say 'load' I mean it. Their concepts of portions are much larger than ours! We tuck in – trying to hold back the thought that today is the day we need to say goodbye for the time being to Osvaldo. Tomorrow early we fly out, so it has been decided that Silvia will come and take him back at lunchtime. We go to the pool and splash about, then go up to our room and get him ready. We have brought a Winnie the Pooh rucksack into which we have packed photo albums of us and toys and things like scarves and wrappers that smell of us.

Silvia arrives and we go down to the taxi: Ossie a sturdy little figure in shorts, T-shirt and sandshoes with his backpack on his back, holding Silvia's hand as he gets in the taxi. He doesn't turn to look at us as the taxi leaves – our hearts are broken. I don't know that anyone who has not been through a similar situation can comprehend the mixture of guilt and sadness that overwhelms you. You keep on thinking there must have been something else you could have done to avoid this situation – some other person to get hold of and appeal to, some string to pull, some tactic to try. Obviously you are a failure – you are leaving your son behind for an unknown length of time and separating him from his sister – you know they are brother and sister because you have seen them together, whatever genetics or so-called experts may say. Meanwhile you have a wife and daughter to look after and get home happy and safe. So you suck it up and get on with things – but the feeling will never leave you and in the deep, dark moments of difficult nights it comes back to haunt you and remind you that you can never be sure of the damage you have allowed to happen.

Early next morning we set off to the airport to fly home. Guillermo and family are there with last minute gifts for us and for the UK family with the twins. We struggle to find somewhere to pack them and off we go. We have chosen to fly KLM because we have been told they are very child friendly. We are given a set of four seats in the centre of the aircraft so that Veronica can lie down across the middle two seats and we can sit at either end. Bottles are heated immediately we ask; toys and colouring kits emerge without being requested; blankets and pillows are in abundance. All the team are so supportive we feel we could not have had a better start on our journey home as a family. After changing planes in Schipol we get back to Heathrow to be met by my sister who drives us home.

A family of three

So here we are with all the bags and suitcases in the hall – coats strewn around and a new encumbrance, the stroller, taking its position at the end of the hallway. After that vital first cup of proper English tea I am ready to collapse so am sent up to bed while Elly does a last bottle and puts Veronica in her cot. Unfortunately, by the time they get upstairs, I am snoring loud enough to make the room shake, so Elly has to struggle to drag the cot through into the children's bedroom and goes to sleep there with Veronica – some homecoming!

The next morning is our first as a family at home. It feels great, our neighbours and relatives are taking their cues from us about how soon to visit and we are heeding the wisdom of those who have gone before us and trying to keep a lid on things. But the best of intentions get diluted, and my sister and her family and my mum just have to drop by, and Vero plays to the crowd.

Our lovely Irish neighbours also drop in just for a moment to share in our happiness. We call all of our friends who have been with us on our adoption journey so far, and let them know we are back. Photos are developed and sent off around the world to friends and relations in Croatia, the US, Japan, Argentina, New Zealand and Scotland.

We do all the necessary paperwork, informing our local authority that we have brought Veronica home and inviting them to carry out their statutory social work visits – in fact they don't come to see us for over two years despite our best efforts to chase them. Perhaps more importantly we get her registered with our doctor and arrange for the health visitor to come to the house. The health visitor is a great find. She immediately looks through the records and carries out her own tests. She makes referrals to all the specialists to look at Veronica's developmental issues and especially the fact that at 18 months she is not walking and her co-ordination and fine motor skills are poor. We have noticed (not surprisingly) that her skin is very dehydrated from the flight, and she looks like a lizard in places, so the district nurse gets us to smother her in E45 cream, especially after her bath. This turns into a nightly massage session, which we carry on for years.

We carried on getting to know each other. We had a small photo album of pictures of Ossie, which we regularly looked at together. Veronica was obviously very attached to him and would constantly ask to see it. Silvia had told us that, because she had been so poorly when she came into her care, Veronica had never slept in a cot but always in a bed. She made her preferences quite clear at the end of day one, and the cot was disassembled and never put in another appearance. Veronica had a bed with a guard to keep her safe and slept happily in it from then on. Getting her into it was a different matter. She wanted to have lots of cuddle time to allow her to drift off and no, you could not leave her to go to sleep by herself. Such dereliction of duty was strictly frowned upon and was greeted with crescendos of howls.

Feeding was pretty simple – so long as you had the time. In fact that was pretty much the case for everything in those early days and weeks. Veronica was not a child to be hurried into anything – even something she wanted to do – and nothing has changed much since!

One of the things that makes adoption so very different is that instead of starting with a newborn who cannot really do much, and for whom you can make all the decisions, you start with someone who is already well on the way to forming their own character. Communications can take a while to get sorted, but even so we parents are given our marching orders. Veronica knew what she wanted, how she wanted things done and when, and found ways to make sure she got it.

We went off to see a specialist to see why she seemed to be slow in walking and had poor motor skills. He carried out a number of tests and came back to us with his conclusions. He said, 'if you think of the scale of normal bendiness as being from here to here' holding his hands about a foot apart 'well, then, Veronica is somewhere over here' holding his hands eighteen inches apart 'in the very bendy end of the spectrum. She has to use a lot more effort just to keep her legs straight and stand up – oh, and she probably needs glasses.'

Well, that explained a lot of things – especially her ability to fall over from a static position! So we researched what we could do and Elly and Vero joined lots of toddlers' activity, music and motion groups and so on. She also went to have her eyes tested and sure enough part of her fine motor skills testing results were down to the fact she couldn't really see what she was looking at.

Of course, while these early lessons were being learnt, we were struggling to keep Ossie's case in motion. His paperwork was progressing and it looked like we might even be able to get him home for Christmas – just six months after Veronica.

This was also the time when we were able to remain quite cocooned as a family and work on understanding and developing our relationships – as a couple as well as with Veronica – and to reflect on our preparation for intercountry adoption.

I suppose that the easiest way I can sum up what I have learned is to say that you need to be able to commit 100 per cent to being part of a family whose identity and values are cross-cultural – in our case Croatian English Guatemalan Japanese Scottish – and that all these heritages are equally valid and valued but differently reflected.

We did huge amounts of reading and preparation before we decided on the country for our adoption. We read and discussed a lot more as we went through the home study.

What follows is a collection of some of the thoughts that emerged and formed the basis of our moving forward. By this time I was an active member of an international e-group specialising in adoption from Guatemala (Guatemala-adopt). For the last nine years I have been co-moderator. Some of the points are made in response to issues raised by others.

- Adoption is not a right for parents – having a family is a right for children and adoption may be the way to achieve that for them. Adoptive parents are the adults in the relationship and need to behave as such – they need to lose any sense of entitlement.
- Intercountry adoptive parents do not have the right to tell any other country how to behave or suggest they should release more of their children to us.
- If you cannot accept the culture, customs, food, weather, people or any other aspect of another country then please do not consider adopting from there. That country is going to be part of your life for evermore and YOU need to support your child

in developing a positive self-image based on their birth culture.

- Do not deny racism (in fact, look into yourself and be aware of the role it plays in your own make up and your life story). Do something about it within your own sphere of influence. If your child will be seen as part of a minority, it is not enough to say 'we love you just the way you are'.
- Accept that grief and loss will be part of your and your child's life for ever – the best you can hope for is to be able to share the burden.
- "Saviour mentality" is not for adoptive parents. If you think 'I am saving this poor orphan' at any time, please stop your adoption process and do something else.
- Find out about all the potential health and mental health issues that affect children adopted from overseas. Do not be an ostrich.
- Prepare for the worst and hope for the best.
- Be aware that intercountry adoption is a business and financial matters are very relevant.
- Do your homework on agencies, processes, procedures and the law. Do not ignore people who describe bad experiences just because others have had positive ones.
- Remember some people suffer from adoption amnesia – especially in the early "honeymoon" period.
- And finally ... if it sounds too good to be true... it is.

Weeks pass as we get on with settling down with Veronica – working out the long-term issues and trying to find solutions for the more immediate ones. There are no doubts that her difficult start in life has had consequences – she is quite significantly delayed both in terms of her physical abilities – at 18 months she is barely toddling and certainly not walking – and also in her intellectual and emotional development. However, there are lots of positives – she has formed strong attachments to both of us and she is a happy and loving little girl.

If there is a downside it is that Elly cannot put her down – she loves being carried around all the time and hates being left anywhere by herself for even a few seconds. This is putting quite a strain on Elly's arms and wrists and back – having an 18-month-old "cling-on" is not easy. Any lack of contact provokes tears and screams. Looking back, I don't know why we never tried the sling option – in Japan all babies are carried "*ombu*" in a long scarf arrangement – I had done it myself and so had Elly. But Elly persevered with Veronica welded to her hip for a long time before she gradually became accustomed to the idea of actually doing some of the work herself by crawling and walking. We knew she had always been very close to Silvia's mother, and we suspected that she had probably been carried on her back in the traditional Guatemalan way and probably for longer than normal because of her slow development. It probably encouraged a reluctance to walk that still persists today!

Meanwhile, Ossie is still working his way through the court procedures and his birth mother, "M", is being incredibly brave and co-operating as much as she can. She has, since Ossie came into the programme, met a new partner and they now have a son, Ossie's half-brother. Guillermo, our lawyer, has had a long discussion about whether she is now in a position to take care of Ossie, but it is clear that, for whatever reason, she is not going back on her decision. So the process continues until finally we get the fantastic news that the court has approved the adoption – a few bureaucratic procedures and it is all over – and a few more weeks and it will be Christmas and days afterwards the beginning of a new Millennium!!

Elly and I again discuss the best way to handle this –

Veronica has been home less than six months and found the journey hard. It seems to make no sense to expose her to the rigours of two long journeys to Guatemala and back as well as huge disruptions to her routine. We don't both want to leave her as that might trigger all sorts of understandable concerns of being abandoned again. So it is decided that I will go out to Guatemala by myself to bring Ossie home – we have already signed all the necessary papers at the British Consulate together – and hopefully before the deadline when the Embassy closes for Christmas; due to fears of the "millennium bug" it will not be opening again till mid-January.

Second trip to Guatemala

So, in mid December 1999, I depart from Heathrow on the long journey to Guatemala City. This time the nerves are even worse. In the months since we last saw Ossie, I have been thinking more and more about how he may respond to the way we swept in, "kidnapped" his sister, and having shown him a glimpse of the possibilities to come, returned him to his foster carer – yet another rejection. I am sure that is how I would have reacted – I would have become really resentful and oppositional. Will he hate me, or want to punish me in some way for his sorrow and pain? Darkened cabins on long distance flights are good places for letting your dark thoughts flower in terrible places. Waiting to go through immigration and customs seems interminable. Again I get the hotel bus to the Marriott and barely have time to dump my bags in the room when I get a call from Guillermo – he and Silvia, the foster carer, are ready to bring Ossie round! There seems to be no point in delaying, so we arrange to meet in the lobby in 20 minutes. I come down in the lift and prowl around, briefly explaining to the staff, who are eying me a bit suspiciously, that I am waiting for my son (actually that sounds really good in Spanish!) whom I haven't seen for some months.

After what seems like ages – but actually according to the Central American concept of time was positively early – here they are, and Ossie zooms into the lobby and runs straight to me holding out his arms to be picked up. I am not even going to try to describe how good that felt – all of the fears and paranoia being washed away with huge waves of relief and love and thanks. Let us just say it was very emotional.

When Ossie and I get done with our mega hug I finally get to say hello and thanks to Guillermo and Silvia. We proceed to the room and have a quick discussion about what needs to be done when. Then far too quickly, Silvia says she is off and will bring Ossie's things around tomorrow but here is a bag with pyjamas and clean clothes for the morning. Guillermo also makes his excuses and we are alone: just Ossie and I.

Forewarned by our first time with him, I have brought lots of toys and amusements – but they are not familiar and don't seem to do the trick at all. So we revert to the basics – running up and down the hotel corridors, laughing and playing ball. As we go down for supper we find what was to be the best diversion ever – an oversize Christmas tree decoration on the hotel's 40-foot Christmas tree, which, when you get close, turns into a funny fir face and "sings" Christmas carols. When Ossie is in my arms he is just the right height to trigger this device, and if we lean close to it enough times, we can hear its full repertoire – and if we do it enough times we can go through them all twice or even three times!! This becomes a necessity every time we go through the hotel lobby for whatever reason! The staff behind the huge reception desk think it is great and encourage him; but *they* don't have to carry him, he is a fair old lump. Ossie is just weeks short of his third birthday and is a solid chap – I am used to carrying Veronica, a year younger and a fair bit slighter – but I soon learn.

Again we go though the rounds: birth certificate,

passport and then the birth mother interview at the British Embassy, which has been delayed so that I can be there. Meeting "M" again is emotional – especially as I am holding Ossie and she has Ossie's younger brother with her. We go into the Torre International, the glass-fronted skyscraper, which houses the British Embassy and into the lift. It is obvious that "M" is anxious, and it emerges that not only is this the first time she has ever been in a building with more than one floor, she has most definitely never been in anything like a lift. She deals with it with remarkable courage – showing an understandable reluctance to come too close to the all-glass outside walls which, 14 floors up, offer fantastic panoramic but vertiginous views, and seem remarkably insubstantial. She goes into the interview with the consul holding Ossie and leaving his brother with me. At that moment I feel like "family". I am sure there is nothing to worry about but it is a relief when they come out and the consul says he will be applying for entry clearance later that day.

Since this is an opportunity not to be missed, I invite Guillermo and "M" to have something to eat – I know she has a long bus trip back to the town near where she lives. So off we go to Pollo Campero, Guatemala's own home-grown fast food joint. Just as an aside, it really is excellent food and something that Guatemalans are rightfully proud of, and with luck a franchise will soon be opened in the UK. While we talk, we are able to share more about ourselves and our plans and hopes and futures, and I am able to promise that we will be bringing Ossie back to see her and the rest of our family in Guatemala. I know she understands and believes that it will happen.

Ossie and I go back to our hotel and start the long wait for London to send through the entry clearance – the visa to let me bring Ossie home to London. Days pass, during which I get to know the consul and his staff – or perhaps it would be more accurate to say that they get sick of the sight and sound of me. But to give them their due, all the officials we have contact with are concerned and understanding.

The Consulate is closing at midday on the 23rd of December and is not due to reopen until mid January because there is panic about the alleged "millennium bug". The days running up to this deadline slide past without any news good or bad. I am having fun with Ossie but it gets very claustrophobic when you don't dare move far because you are waiting for a call, and there are not many safe and child-friendly things to do in the immediate vicinity. On top of that I am missing Elly and Veronica desperately; we have become such a tight little unit over the past few months. Finally, just after 11 o'clock on the 23rd, I receive a call from the consul. The relevant department in London is happy for the entry clearance to be given but will not be able to do the paperwork before Christmas. Now according to all the rules and regulations, an entry permit cannot be issued without the right paperwork. I am, and will be, forever grateful to the consul who took matters into his own hands and decided it was not right for us to be kept away from home any longer waiting for London to catch up with its paperwork – 'get over here straight away' he said, 'we are about to close'.

I tuck Ossie under my arm and go through the eight lanes of traffic of Avenida Reforma like Micky Skinner in his heyday – nothing is going to stop me. I rush into the Embassy, past all the guards who are looking decidedly askance at the mad Englishman (scarily they were holding guns), and the consul and his team are waiting to do the necessary. To say they went way beyond the call of duty is an understatement: not only did they sort out all the UK paperwork in double quick time, but they phoned through to the KLM office to ask them to wait for us and ordered a taxi to get us there as quickly as possible. I wrote to the Consulate when we got home, but even now, years later, I want them to know that I am forever indebted to those true professionals and diplomats who took the extra step to help. So Ossie and I now have a visa in his passport and after a short but suitably crazy taxi ride two tickets for the plane leaving on the 24th, arriving on the 25th December. We rush back to the Marriott to tell Elly we will be back on Christmas Day!!

I then start to take stock of things. Some things are easy – I call Guillermo and tell him the good news and we arrange to meet for a farewell early evening drink. I look around and realise that Ossie has shorts and sand shoes and T-shirts …and in 48 hours or so we will be landing in Heathrow at the end of December! So we rush out again before the shops shut to get him some winter clothes and shoes. Long cord trousers, check shirt, sweater, jeans jacket, socks and we look for appropriate shoes; we find some beautiful leather Mickey Mouse boots. Now for whatever reason, and it may be that they are his first ever pair of new shoes, or it may be the particular attraction of Mickey, but Ossie is in love with these boots. He walks around hugging them as we say goodbye to Guillermo, and they are beside him as he has his supper; much as he likes our waitress, she is not allowed to do more than admire them from afar, definitely no touching! We go up to our room, Ossie has his bath and after he is in his pyjamas insists on putting his boots on to go to bed, and the photograph of him fast asleep in his Mickey Mouse boots still hangs in his bedroom.

The next day we are off early to the airport, which is heaving with people. We get checked in, but even with a stroller (which is actually a pain in the posterior as I have to put it through every one of the four or five scanning/x-ray machines), I seem to be weighed down with all the hand luggage I am carrying. Ossie thinks it is a great laugh to rush off every time we get to an inspection and my hands are full of documents and the officials are being particularly officious. My stress levels are rising very rapidly and I am definitely not enjoying this journey. We finally get to board the plane and it is seriously overloaded. Ossie is on my lap and even the rear facing crew seats seem to have passengers in them. My heart sinks – how many hours of this will we have to put up with? I try to stay jolly and help Ossie with the weird sensations of flying, which, it should be noted, he dealt with stoically except for being forced to stay sitting when he wanted to go and play.

After a few hours – it feels like days – we land in Mexico City. Because the plane is being refuelled we all have to get off, and half an hour or so later we are called to board again. But this time there is no crowd, there is a mere smattering of us, in fact there seems to be more crew than passengers! So the captain wishes us a merry Christmas and invites us all into first class. Ossie very soon settles into the lifestyle he obviously wishes to become accustomed to. A huge seat with his own TV screen (less common than now), cabin staff who seem to be there solely for his amusement and to do his bidding, with food and drink in constant supply. Toys, drawing kits...the treats seem endless. The wonderful crew even wrap up a bottle of very good champagne in linen napkins for me to take to Elly. Time passes quickly as Ossie and I snuggle and snore our way towards Schipol – and yes Ossie did and does snore.

We get to Amsterdam and disembark and it is a very eerie and strange place, the airport seems to be shut. Way off in the distance is a light but all the rest is in darkness except for the dim glow of the emergency lighting. We look for the outbound flights – there is only one, ours, to London. Somewhere over the Atlantic we have crossed over to Christmas Day and it hasn't even registered. A couple of hot chocolates later and we go off to find our connecting flight. No problem, we get on board – there are probably about 10 or 12 of us now – get ourselves seated and wait for take off. Surely no reason for delays on a day like this? But we have not counted on the fickle finger of fate. The Captain announces that the ground radar is not working; they will try to get a technician, but it is Christmas... Half an hour later he is on again to say 'no luck' and we will have to change planes. There is no shortage of aircraft, as it would appear that most of the KLM fleet is in Amsterdam for the holidays and all we can see out of the windows are rows and rows of KLM planes. Forty-five minutes later, having helped shift the baggage, we are in our new, not broken plane, and ready to leave.

Meanwhile, back in the UK, Elly calls the British Airport Authority to see if there are any delays before she sets off for the short journey to Heathrow from our home in Chiswick. She gets a curt and rather testy reply to the effect that it is Christmas Day and there are no planes in the air, so of course there aren't any delays. When she gets to the airport, there is a sign that we will be delayed by over an hour! Let's just say she was not amused!

We land without further incident and set off for immigration. In the huge hall usually brimming with people, there is one solitary immigration officer on the non-UK/EU nationals side. No one has removed the system of rails used to guide people waiting in the queue, so Ossie and I zig-zag our way to his desk. He reads the entry clearance stamp "for the purpose of adoption" in Ossie's passport, stamps it carefully, gets up from his chair, walks round the desk and says, 'Welcome to the UK, young man' and shakes Ossie's hand. Manners maketh man – top man.

We pick up the luggage and head out to the arrivals area where Elly and Veronica are waiting. Huge hugs all round. Elly and I are probably too emotionally and physically exhausted to really appreciate the moment. We should have been screaming our heads off with joy: we are home!

Veronica obviously remembers Ossie and makes it clear she is very happy to see him again. Ossie is a bit overwhelmed by the attention.

By now it is late on Christmas Day and we agree to hold Christmas again the next day so that we can all enjoy the whole thing properly – but we have already had the best Christmas present we could ever have hoped for: our family is complete at last.

The next day Ossie and I are suffering a little from jet lag and travelling for over 24 hours the previous two days, so we get a bit of a lie in. But then the girls wake us up and we all set to, learning more and more about each other and being a family. Veronica is quite amazing. She knows exactly who Ossie is and wants to take up where they left off. He is lying in his bed still drowsy and not really ready to face the day. Vero brings some cars and a wooden train set over to him and pushes a car into his hand. He takes it and tucks it behind his back. She hands him another and he places it with the first one, out of sight behind him. This goes on with all the cars and the whole train set. They have made it into a game, and the two of them are looking into each other's eyes from inches away and smiling broadly. Ossie gets up, and they get the "tea service" out and start playing tea parties. All of this, with Elly and me just looking on in amazement and delight, and the video camera diligently recording. After a while they seem to notice us and we all get to play, and then move on to breakfast.

The day goes past in a blur: all the usual Christmas things, presents, tree (but disappointingly without a fir head singing carols), turkey, trimmings and Christmas pudding. Elly's mum, Jean, is down from Scotland and loving it all. I walk around with this silly grin on my face all the time. I keep seeing our house with my wife and our children in it and it still seems to be an incredible dream. We have been working and hoping for this for so long that it is almost too hard to take in that it has actually happened. Watching Ossie and Vero playing together, sharing their food, cuddling, running around, building and knocking down towers of wooden bricks, having a bath – it is almost too much happiness for any human being. As we lie down in bed together at the end of the day, Elly and I struggle to find any words and just hug and touch to share our joy. What a Christmas!!

PART 2

Yellow: the colour of a child's laugh

A few days later and it is the millennium. For us the new age has already begun, but we watch the festivities on the television, cocooned as we are in our family. But January also brings with it the children's birthdays. Ossie's birthday is two days after Veronica's, so for two days they are the same age – this will have increasing importance as time passes. We have a long discussion about whether or not to have a party. Ossie has just got home and we don't want to push things along too fast. Elly's sister and her youngest son are also arriving from Japan to see Jean, whose birthday is two days before Veronica's, and who will be celebrating her 80th. So we decide we will go for it in a fairly low-key way, and call a couple of other families who have adopted from Guatemala, and who have been a really strong support along the way. We also call a photographer friend of ours to take some photos to mark Jean's 80th and the foundation of our family.

The whole day goes amazingly well. The photographer works around us, and even the posed pictures look natural.

Veronica knows all of the children who come to the party but Ossie also gets stuck in and enjoys playing with them. He is obviously used to playing with lots of other children. We know that all of Silvia's family are foster carers: Silvia, her mother, sister and sisters-in-law. They all live together and the children all play together. The party is a success and everyone seems happy.

I took the rest of January off to work from home on the computer when the kids were asleep. Elly had decided to take leave from school until we felt that the children were ready. The day came when I was to go back to the office. We had been working up to this, trying to explain that I would go out but would definitely be back for supper. We all ate early around the table together and still do. When I went out to work that morning, Ossie stood looking at the closed door for ages – it broke my heart when Elly told me that evening. We discussed the options: do I leave early so he doesn't see me go, or make it a more formal affair? We decided on the latter, so I would say goodbye to Ossie and Veronica and promise them I would be back as quickly as possible, but definitely by suppertime. I got lots of kisses and cuddles as I left and even more when I came home.

Again we were able to rely on the support of the health visitor to get Ossie assessed and any problems identified, although at this stage there did not seem to be any. Like many children adopted from Guatemala, his diet had not been optimal, but he soon lost some of the chubbiness as he raced around like any normal three-year-old boy.

We started to think about playgroups, nursery and school. Our local primary school seemed like an obvious choice for reception and onwards. It was really close, all the neighbourhood children went there, so it was very mixed racially, with a single form entry small enough to ensure no child "disappeared" into the system. In short it ticked all the boxes. For nursery, we wanted a gentler start. We felt the children were ready for this step but we wanted to make sure that it was going to be a nurturing, caring environment with not too many children or too much pressure.

We found the most amazing nursery run by a group of nuns, most of whom were Italian, with only a dozen or so children, and about 15 minutes walk from home (or pushing the buggy since Veronica was not really up to the walk yet). The food was home cooked and the love and care was unbelievable – it was like being looked after by a group of Italian grandmothers. The other children were of many different ethnicities, which we felt was important.

So when Veronica was three and Ossie was four, the children started nursery and Elly went back to school. They went part-time for a few days but soon showed they were more than happy to stay for longer. My office was just a few minutes walk away, so I could get there if there were any problems, but none arose. I walked them to the nursery in the morning and Elly collected them after school. In between the children had a great time, made friends, and were spoiled rotten!

As required, we had notified the local authority that both Veronica and Ossie had come home. The law has changed now, but at the time there was no time limit for the local authority to check on the children and to write the report that was necessary before we could "re-adopt" them in the UK. In the meanwhile they were in a sort of legal limbo. Since the UK did not recognise the adoptions in Guatemala, we did not have any legal parental responsibility. We repeatedly contacted the local authority only to be told they did not have any resources to visit us and to start the report. So we carried on without official supervision; the local authority had no idea about the wellbeing of the children or about their care, education or indeed anything at all.

Because Veronica's visa was running out (she had been with us for nearly a year), we decided to celebrate our

"Family Day", the anniversary of the day we met the children, by going to Calais on the ferry, going out for lunch, doing some early Christmas shopping and on the way back asking the immigration officer to extend both children's visas for six months and so to synchronise them. Before we left we had to get a letter from the local authority giving us permission to go, which, after a lot of persuasion, they gave us. All round, the day was a great success.

However, six months later we had to do the same thing once more, but this time we were warned we would not be allowed to get the children's visas renewed via this route again. The next time we would have to go to the Home Office department in Lunar House in Croydon. Sure enough, we had made no progress six months later, so I set off to Croydon on the tram. I had been warned to make sure I got there early – but despite arriving before 7am there was a huge queue ahead of me. It was a miserable day, cold and drizzling and we waited outside without any shelter until 9am, when the doors opened and we were allowed in. We were a very mixed group, but most people were not British and did not have English as their first language. The staff were incredibly rude and dismissive and seemed to have that very English belief that speaking louder (and patronisingly) will help people to understand. It opened my eyes to the way in which many people of colour were being treated by officialdom in this country. I was ashamed and disgusted, not only by the reality, but also that I had been so naïve as to not expect it. Actually it was a salutary lesson that has informed my thoughts and actions ever since.

When I got to the head of the queue, having tried to help a few other "queuers" with their incomprehensible and over-complex forms, I handed in our form and the children's passports, tried unsuccessfully to get some confirmation that I had filled it in correctly (we did not seem to fit neatly into any of the categories) and was told to come back at 2pm. I wandered about Croydon for a few hours, which is not as bad as it sounds, and returned expecting to meet the immigration officer, pick up the passports and go home. Instead, I was told that the officer had decided to get the immigration record from Dover regarding the last time we had entered the country to see if there were any comments on it, and he wanted to investigate the status of the children and why they were in our care! Oh and this might take six or more months, but in the meanwhile the children's passports would be confiscated.

I was infuriated. The arrogance and ignorance of the man was appalling and the complete lack of insight was inexcusable from someone in his position. I made myself very clear: we were only in this situation because our local authority had failed to carry out its responsibilities to enable us to "re-adopt" in the UK. The delays were not our fault. I persuaded him to phone the council and speak to the duty officer in the adoption team, who was able, after long and at times heated discussion, to look up our file, confirm we had done everything by the book and that the council was responsible for the fact that we were having to renew the children's visas for the third time. The officer went off to meet with his manager. The manager came down to talk to me. They got the message that I was articulate and was not going to let them get away with not giving me the visas – so they did and I went home. But I could see that a lot of the other applicants were not as articulate and confident as I was, and I feared their outcomes were going to be less happy than mine. I was determined to make sure that our children would be prepared for this sort of situation.

Eventually, after Veronica had been with us for over two years, we were allocated a trainee social worker to visit us and write the report, which had to be submitted to the court as part of our adoption application. She was doing this with a marked degree of reluctance because she felt she had not been prepared for the job and was not being supported in doing it. So her visits were often short, the gaps between them were protracted, and her disquiet about her lack of management support became more and more of an issue.

Finally, after about a year, she announced that she had completed her report and that a date had been set for a directions hearing at the local Magistrates' Court, which, as it happened, was one of the designated courts for hearing such adoption cases. Fantastic, we thought, not much further to go...and then we received our copy of the report. The best that can be said was that it seemed like a framework on which to base a report. It was full of factual errors and the language and spelling made it hard to understand. We called the social worker and invited her to come round for a chat about the report – and perhaps bring it on a disk. This she duly did. She was visibly upset as I suppose she expected a negative reaction from us. But instead we suggested that since she had not had a lot of help, perhaps we could work on it together.

So Elly and the social worker sat down at the table to go through the hard copy and I loaded the disk and we started to go though correcting and improving the report, agreeing each section as we went. In the end we had something we all felt was correct and a fair representation of our situation. I printed it out, we signed it and sat back to wait for the directions hearing just before Christmas.

Since we had been led to believe that this was predominantly an administrative exercise, where the Judge determined whatever additional information or actions he or she required, we did not take the children out of nursery. Elly and I dressed up and went to meet our social worker at the entrance to the court. Fifteen minutes later a different social worker arrived and said she was standing in for our social worker. We went into the court. A few minutes later the Judge came in, with our report in his hand. He sat down, we sat down, he thanked the borough for the quality of the report, and said that on the basis of the report he was minded to grant the adoption. He stood up, we stood up and he went out.

We sat there stunned and confused and frankly not entirely sure what had happened. We asked the social worker and she was not sure either, so we went to the Clerk of the court who confirmed that our adoption had indeed been completed and the paperwork would be sent through shortly.

Whilst this was wonderful news – the process was finally over after nearly six years – it was also a bit of an anti-climax. No robes, no ceremony, no children present and no idea of what had just happened! We set about letting all our families and friends know, and it turned out that one friend we had met on our preparation course knew the Judge quite well. Consequently, a few days later we were given an invitation to come back to see the Judge again early in the New Year. This time he was dressed up in all his finery and allowed us to take photos in the court under the great seal, with the children sitting on his desk with him. Another top man.

Full parental responsibility
We were now able to assume full parental responsibility, get the children registered with new birth certificates showing us as the children's parents, and subsequently get British passports for them.

Ossie was coming to the end of his time in nursery and we had to start thinking about primary school. We had got him a place at the local school we wanted, which was a lovely single storey building in a large playground. The two teachers who were going to be job sharing in his reception year made an appointment to come and see us at home.

For some time at the get-togethers of the UK adoption

support groups and online, we had been following the discussions of how to introduce adoption-related topics to teachers. We printed out guides and exercises that we could offer them to minimise the impact on Ossie. For example, instead of asking children to make a family tree, as is often done, another model that has been suggested, and that we have found to work well, is that children draw a simple house and in each door or window they put the names or draw the faces of people who are important in their lives – whatever their actual relationship might be.

School and adoption

When your child starts school it can be a challenging time for all concerned – your child, yourself and the teacher. We can make this transition easier by helping teachers with information and vocabulary that they in turn can pass on to other pupils. Good communication is going to be the key – with the teachers, of course, but also listening very closely to our children and helping them find positive solutions. We have to leave the decisions about when and how the subject of family formation, including adoption, is introduced into the classroom. However, it has been our experience that when we have been proactive by helping to point out some options and resources, our children's teachers have responded positively.

Obviously you need to keep up with your child's academic performance; some studies show that up to 40 per cent of intercountry adopted children have some special educational needs. Being aware of problems as early as possible and helping to get the necessary support is critical to their self-esteem. Become as involved as you can, attend all parent–teacher meetings and school events. If you can, become a class parent representative or become active in the PTA. Your children need to know you are doing what you can to support them.

Unfortunately much of the information circulating

about adoption is either inaccurate, old fashioned or downright discriminatory. So even teachers who are knowledgeable and those who want to be sensitive about adoption will benefit from having a basis to start from.

Information for teachers

Here is a sample letter and some information you might want to share with your child's teachers:

> *Dear (teacher's name)*
>
> *We just wanted to make sure that you know that our family was formed through adoption. There are some great resources about adoption, which I will be happy to share with you at any time. In the meantime I thought it might be helpful if we share a few ideas, some answers to common questions and some thoughts about projects children in your class might get involved with.*
>
> *We are sure you would agree that there are many kinds of blended families in our modern society and that adoption is one valid way of building a family. We have learned that families are created through mutual love, caring and respect and not solely through genetic connections. Thank you for helping to communicate this to XXX's classmates.*
>
> *With best wishes*

Background information on intercountry adoption and child's country of origin

Intercountry adoption is a valid means to help a child fulfil their right to grow up "in a family environment in an atmosphere of happiness, love and understanding". You might like to look at www.adoptivefamilies.com/ articles.php?aid=467 for ideas to use in the classroom.

Common questions and some possible answers

Who/where are XXX's real parents?
XXX has two sets of real parents. Mum (name) and Dad (name) who are raising him/her here in the UK and his/her birth parents in (country of birth) as he/she was born to them.

Where is XXX from?
XXX is from (name of town). He/she was born in (country of birth) and is now British.

Why doesn't XXX look like her mum or dad?
XXX was born in (country of birth) and he/she was adopted by his/her parents when he/she was little. His/her parents are British and so is he/she now.

Does XXX speak (language of country of birth)?
Either yes/quite a lot/a bit

or

No. XXX came to the UK when he/she was little and he/she was not speaking any language at that time. So he/she has learned the language of the country he/she is growing up in.

Did it cost a lot to adopt him/her?
There are lots of costs in adoption for agencies and professionals to cover the legal and social work involved in intercountry adoption, but no one pays or gets paid for the child. All children are priceless.

Did his/her parents buy him/her?
No. They had to pay lots for agencies and professionals to cover the legal and social work costs involved, but no one can buy a child.

Why didn't his/her birth family want him/her? Didn't they love him/her?
They probably loved him/her very much, but it was not possible for them to care for XXX at that time. XXX

needed a family who could take care of and love him/her forever and his/her parents were chosen to do that. Adoptions always happen for grown-up reasons and never because of something a child does.

Potentially problematic assignments

The complexity of family composition is increasing as our society changes. Class assignments now need to reflect the wide variety of family patterns to allow for all the possible non-traditional families a child can belong to. Otherwise a child may not only feel different and out of place, or even excluded, but also not be or feel able to complete the work, with consequent loss of self-esteem or confidence.

Family tree

Rather than asking children to complete their family tree, which is almost impossible to do meaningfully if you are adopted, it might be better to help children understand the variety of family structures by other means.

You could draw a picture of a house and ask the children to populate it with people who are part of their family or who are important to them. You might suggest that the downstairs windows and door are for the people who you live with or see all the time and the upstairs are for those you see less often.

Another idea would be a "family wheel" with concentric circles and spokes to help divide it into convenient areas with the child at the hub. Here the first circle out from the hub might be the people you live with, the next circle for people you see all the time and the outer circle for those you see less often.

This is also an opportunity to help children understand the complexities of their classmates' backgrounds in an inclusive and non-judgemental way.

Bring in a baby photo

This can be a real problem for those who do not have any – which might include fostered or adopted as well as unaccompanied refugee or asylum-seeking children.

To illustrate genetics, growth and change, a child could be asked to bring in a series of photos of any family member or friend, or any famous person, showing them at various ages. If photos of family or friends are not available, then the internet has them in abundance of celebrities.

Trace the origins of your eye colour

Some children will not be able to trace inherited characteristics and could therefore be made to feel different. It might be helpful to use a common source for the data (perhaps the teacher themselves).

Write the story of your life

Rather than presenting a child with the choice of telling a part of their story they do not wish to share, or may not know, or which brings out painful feelings and memories, it is better to ask them to write about a favourite event or experience.

Celebrate Mother's or Father's Day

For children with blended families this can raise painful memories – or they may need to produce multiples! It may be better to ask them to make cards for the people who look after them and let them decide how many, for whom, and how to address the recipients.

More details

For a more detailed resource document please look at *A Teachers Guide to Adoption* by Robin Hilborn, which can be obtained for free on the internet.

Adoption language

The following is adapted from the OASIS Media Guide:

Adoptive families are normal families. It is so easy – and yet so dangerous and potentially damaging – for people (even inadvertently) to portray adopted children or adults as being somehow "different" and not "regular" family members.

The biggest danger is to make assumptions and to overlay stereotypes.

We need to realise and act on the fact that poor use of adoption language impacts harshly on ordinary families who happen to have been formed by adoption.

Fundamentally, the only time the fact that a person was adopted should be mentioned is where it is essential to the meaning of a situation – and in this case its relevance should be made clear, as with ability, gender and race issues. A child who joined a family through adoption is simply a child of that family – and deserves the dignity of being described as such. Adoption is an event in a person's life: it is not a characteristic or trait.

In situations where it is relevant, it is best to use the past tense as in "he was adopted in 1998" or "he was adopted aged three".

Adoptive parents are just parents – father, mother, dad, mum, papa, etc. An adopted person's other family members are similarly brothers, sisters, grandparents, cousins, aunts, etc.

The use of the words "real" and "natural" to describe genetic parents is fraught with difficulty. Adoptive parents are not fictitious, unsubstantial or unnatural.

Generally speaking, it is easiest to refer to biological family as "birth parents, birth-mother or birth-father, etc." Children who are available for adoption are usually not orphans and thus it is misleading to describe them as such, except where this fact has been established.

No child should ever be described as "unwanted" and the phrases "abandoned" or "given up" are also problematic and should be avoided if possible. Depending on the circumstances, it is better to be accurate and say "the birth-parents placed the child for adoption" or "the child was placed in an institution" or "the child was taken into care" rather than second guess the reasons for this happening.

The phrase "...could not have a baby of their (or his or her) own" for those with fertility issues is simply wrong as well as being deeply hurtful. Children who enter families through adoption are just as much their parents' "own" as any other child.

The reason people adopt is very rarely relevant – you would hesitate to ask why a couple have undertaken fertility treatment or why they have decided to have a baby – so you should be equally wary of assuming why they have chosen to adopt. There are many ways to create a family and they are all equally valid – there is no second best. Many families have used more than one way to build their families.

Adoptive parents are not abnormally selfless or "good" or "kind".

They (in the most part) are certainly no more saintly than the rest of society.

It should be noted that the same standards apply to all forms of adoption in the UK – domestic, intercountry, transracial, family and friends and that the process is a long, detailed, invasive and intensive one. It certainly does not happen quickly or without a great deal of determination and dedication on the part of the parents.

Both of Ossie's future teachers were obviously very experienced and knowledgeable; they took our suggestions and ideas on board in a very positive way; they understood that we were only offering them resources, not making demands. However, we know that not all teachers react in this way, and some schools can get very defensive. But I must acknowledge that we have had fantastic help. When Ossie was doing social and sex education in year five, his teacher's husband was an adopted person, and she was able to speak meaningfully and sensitively to the class about adoption as a way of building a family, and of some of the issues that can stem from it, without once referring to Ossie's status. It made quite an impact on him that others, outside of the adoption community he knew, could really understand the feelings and thoughts and concerns of adopted people. The materials used for the course acknowledged many different ways of forming families, but this teacher's personal input was crucial to making it successful.

One of the factors that had drawn us to the school and the whole area was its mixed ethnic composition. Again, our reading and discussions had led us to choose environments where our children would not stand out as the only, or one of a few, children of colour. It was an added advantage that there were quite a few "mixed race" marriages in our neighbourhood, which meant it was not "different" for parents not to look like their child.

We were keen to get more direct contact with people who reflected the children's ethnicity, and with primary school would come a definite need for someone to collect Ossie at the end of the school day, which to begin with would be shorter than the nursery day. We decided that it would be a good idea to get a Central or Latin American student to come and live with us, spend time with the children, and be a bit of a role model and source of language and music.

We found a hostel run by nuns (of course!) that specialised in providing a base from which Central and Latin American young women could find home-stays and au pair placements. Over the years we have had quite a few girls come to us from the nuns: mainly Mexican but also two Colombians, and they were all great. Enthusiastic, child friendly, energetic, full of life and enjoyment, they have set really good examples for the children as well as reflecting their colour and ethnicity to a greater or lesser degree.

To help support their language further, we found a really nice Spanish playgroup and the children used to go there every Saturday to sing songs and play games in Spanish. Most of the families were Latin American and from a wide variety of backgrounds. In time we ended up on the committee and helped to organise fundraising as well as the venue and teachers.

So after the summer holidays Ossie went off to primary school and Veronica continued at nursery. Ossie had a great start. He quickly made friends – many of whom remain his friends even now. His physical abilities, especially his hand eye co-ordination and ball skills, meant that he was quickly accepted not only by his contemporaries but also by older boys who wanted him on their team. There is no doubt that boys who are good at sports, especially football, are quickly and easily accepted by the group, even if their academic prowess does not match up. That was certainly the case with Ossie.

Our support network

About this time I started to get more and more involved with the adoption support groups in the UK. The Guatemalan Families Association was set up by an amazing woman to help support families through the process of adopting from Guatemala, and also to provide a social setting for the children and parents to meet, to share their experiences, and to build friendships and relationships. It sent out a short newsletter, which was characterised mainly by its very personal nature. As the membership increased, we moved towards having a committee to expand the services offered. We came up with a number of issues we felt we could address.

The first was to document the adoption process in Guatemala for UK citizens, so that members could be sure about what paperwork they needed and what steps had to be taken in the Guatemalan courts and legal system and subsequently the British Embassy.

Secondly, as well as the established pattern of parties and get-togethers, we introduced an away weekend, to focus on exploring elements of Guatemalan culture in age-appropriate ways and, perhaps more importantly, build peer groups so that all of the children, wherever they lived in the British Isles, would have a friendship group of contemporaries, who shared not only that they were from Guatemala but also that they had been adopted. Over time the cultural weekend has grown to be a fantastic experience for all the children, whatever their age, and one they all look forward to. Obviously the range of activities has changed as the children have grown into young adults, so we now have things like climbing walls and fencing for the older children as well as activity rooms where they can just "hang out". In addition we have "older children only" events like "snow-tubing" and bowling so that they have a chance to get together and chat and exchange ideas and experiences.

Thirdly, we wanted our children to gain a better knowledge and understanding of the country of their birth. It is too easy to characterise it by its Mayan heritage, or to explain everything away by blaming the ravages of the civil war, or the US or the battle between Catholicism and Evangelicalism. It is important for the children to try to get a more balanced view, one that includes positive stories and role models. So for us the role of Pollo Campero, the fast food chicken restaurant, in creating a Guatemalan-born industry that is expanding beyond the country of its birth, based on the quality and popularity of its products, is just as great a triumph as the creation of the magnificent pyramids and squares and plazas of Tikal.

Lastly, we set out to consistently counter the inaccurate

and negative press coverage of Guatemalan adoptions. Whilst no one will pretend that any system, let alone a system in a country as oppressed by corruption and inequality as Guatemala, is perfect, the media reporting of adoptions in Guatemala has at best been sensationalist and at worst embellished beyond any correspondence with the truth. There was also, and still remains, a lot of negativity about intercountry adoption from some United Nations (UN) organisations, despite the fact that it is sanctioned by the UN Resolution on the Rights of the Child and the Hague Convention on Intercountry Adoption. The UK media would talk to us to get our point of view and then quite happily write a story based on complete fiction, which they knew from the facts and references we had provided to be untrue. Unfortunately even when we did get any retractions or apologies, they were too little, too late and it was the one area of endeavour where we did not really make any impact.

However, the friendships we and our children have made over the years are very important to them and us. The activities of the GFA have definitely helped our children with their knowledge and awareness of the country of their birth and thus, in the long term, with their self-image and self-esteem. I believe the value of country-specific support groups cannot be overestimated and I congratulate all the volunteers in all the groups for the efforts they have made and the successes they have achieved in supporting their children.

The other group I have become significantly involved in is OASIS, the largest non-country-specific support group in the UK. My first involvement was to help them with their information leaflet on Guatemala. Up until this time the organisation had probably spent most of its time and effort on educating and informing its members pre-adoption. But as the numbers of children adopted from overseas increased, more and more effort was being put into supporting members and their children post-adoption. One of the main strategies was to bring over the world's best experts, usually from the US, to speak about their areas of expertise. So Holly van Gulden, Dan Hughes and Dana Johnson, among others, have come to talk about attachment, therapeutic parenting, the medical issues and long-term outcomes for adopted people, especially in terms of mental health and educational issues.

OASIS also publishes a really good magazine – *Mosaic*. The content has always been excellent and recently we have also improved the production values so that it looks as good as it reads.

Now, as with so many other organisations, we are able to take advantage of developments in communications and a lot of what we do is done via our website: www.adoptions overseas.org. Increasingly the strategy is to provide more and more content for members to access in this way since it means that funds can be concentrated on providing the information rather than on the means to communicate it.

I believe that the value of support groups cannot be overestimated. The feeling of belonging and comfort that comes from being in a group of people who fundamentally understand where you are coming from, and what you are going through, is invaluable. People with personal experience can understand viscerally – from a deep-seated almost instinctual level. A panel member, who was a social work professional, changed significantly when he became a foster carer. Not that his decisions or actions changed necessarily, but he had walked the walk rather than sympathising or intellectually empathising.

It is important that support groups are not related to the official process, so that things can be shared and revealed without prejudicing your case, and frustrations and anger vented. Conversely, major and minor victories can only be celebrated with those who understand what goes into achieving them.

I think it is also really important that OASIS has always had a very strong moral stance – everyone who has written or helped on information lines has been really careful to be brutally honest about the realities of intercountry adoption, and whilst we have promoted the benefits, we readily acknowledge the negative side as well.

Some thoughts on intercountry adoption

Whilst I am getting ahead of the story, I think this is an apt moment to share more thoughts on intercountry adoption in general and in the UK in particular.

Intercountry adoption is one of those issues that really polarises professionals and society alike. It takes the controversy at the heart of adoption and magnifies it.

Adoption can be seen as the worst form of human exploitation, especially when "race" is brought into the equation in transracial or intercountry adoption. The privileged may be seen as taking the children of the most underprivileged and depriving them of their racial and cultural communities in what may be seen to be a form of colonialism.

At the other extreme, there is a view that transracial and intercountry adoption can be seen as a positive force: the parents reach out to a child in need of a family, without competing for the limited number of children who meet the strict race/culture/class/nation criteria imposed by the first viewpoint. They form families which are stronger for being built across the lines of racial or cultural difference.

As usual, the truth lies somewhere between these two extremes.

There is an alternative approach to adoption that is worthy of consideration.

Elizabeth Bartholet, Professor of Law at Harvard Law School (www.law.harvard.edu/faculty/bartholet/) writes:

> *At present, the law poses as the protector of children, but to a great degree functions as their enemy. The problem*

is that the law focuses only on the negative potential of international adoption and ignores its positive potential. The law addresses the dangers to children and birth parents that might be involved in removing them for adoption abroad, but ignores the dangers to children involved in growing up on the streets or in institutions.

Many supporters of the law seem genuinely unaware of its costs. The common assumption is that more law will mean more protection against abuse for more children. Few recognize that legal procedures designed on paper to protect children against abuse often become in practice legal barriers that deny children the loving homes they need to escape a life of abuse.

There is, of course, a need for law to ensure that children are not improperly taken from their birth parents or transferred to situations in which they will be mistreated or exploited. But the law should also guarantee children the fundamental right to grow up in a nurturing environment. By focusing exclusively on the negative potential of international adoption, the law fails in its overall obligation to serve children's best interests.

I think it is fair to say that this last point describes the attitude of legislators in the UK and also of those who are responsible for implementing the laws. The result is that the UK is way behind any of its European neighbours in the numbers of overseas adoptions. At its peak, Spain, the leading European country for intercountry adoption, adopted 5,541 children from overseas (10.2 children per 100,000 population). The UK peaked at 363 (0.6 per 100,000 population).

Many reasons have been put forward for the very low numbers of intercountry adoptions in the UK. These include:

• the ideological opposition to intercountry

adoption and transracial adoption by local
authority social work departments and
professionals
- the significant delays in bringing forward
  appropriate legislation and regulation
- the ineffective enforcement of the law and
  regulations due to the lack of a separate
  inspectorate and the unwillingness of the Central
  Authority to carry out its duties
- the fact that intercountry adoption is an
  immigration issue
- the lack of experience and expertise in intercountry adoption among professionals

In addition, there are fundamental structural issues. The
UK has had a strong and well-founded system of domestic
adoption, although some aspects of this have been called
into question over recent years and numbers have been in
decline. Because of this, and an unfounded ideological
belief that the same systems need to be applied to both
domestic and intercountry adoption, the UK has tried to
adapt the domestic system to meet the immeasurably
different needs of intercountry adoption. Other countries
have developed the two systems separately and specifically,
and arguably with a great deal more success.

The intercountry adoption system in the UK simply
does not work. There are children out there in the world
for whom intercountry adoption represents their only
chance of a family, which both the UN Convention on the
Rights of the Child and the Hague Convention on
Intercountry Adoption agree is a fundamental human
right, and which comes higher in their agreed hierarchy
than institutional care of any form. The UK system is
denying them that right.

To paraphrase Elizabeth Bartholet: the children are not
a powerful political constituency – they have no voice.

Many of those who claim to speak for them are engaged in political hostilities – or are making grand symbolic political gestures. If they could move beyond these to focus on the situation of those children who are in need of a family, they would see that, for some of the world's children, intercountry adoption is a good solution. And if they could see that, then they could restructure the laws that currently impede adoptions to facilitate them, and ensure that the best interests of such children are given the primacy they deserve.

It may seem impossible but it is a dream I am committed to fighting for.

Learning difficulties

The time then came for Veronica to join Ossie at primary school. Their classes had very different characters; however, both were able to settle in very fast and create strong friendships that endure to this day. There were lots of play dates and our house was often full of children.

It very soon became apparent, as Ossie progressed up the school and Vero started on the academic process, that both of the children had significant learning difficulties. By learning difficulties I mean exactly that – UK style school-based academic learning is very problematic for them, for different reasons.

Both had real difficulties with reading, although Ossie seemed to have a switch to turn on in his head: after a very long while, and quite suddenly, things came together. For Veronica this has never happened. Ossie has aural memory problems and Vero has issues with her short-term working memory.

For both of them this meant that we had to ask for lots of support from the school – which we had to fight for since all resources in education are scarce – and put in place some private arrangements as well.

One of the things we found (and find) frustrating is that

despite the superficial interest and commitment to the different learning styles (visual, auditory and kinaesthetic), nothing has changed fundamentally, especially when it comes to exams.

For example, mental maths was an oral exercise – which Ossie always failed at. When we managed to persuade the teacher to also use flash cards, he was suddenly a success: his problem was he couldn't remember all the components of the question when he heard it; but when he saw it, even for just a fraction of a second, he could do the maths.

For Veronica maths is a minefield – she is actually very capable if the question is written down in numbers. But it seems that maths tests are also English tests now, with long complex questions, often containing "tricks". So the time it takes her to properly read the questions means she has run out of time to actually answer more than just a few. When she has a reader (not often, unfortunately) she does very well.

OASIS carried out a small-scale questionnaire into the numbers of children adopted from overseas who had learning difficulties. Given that the number in the general population of children in primary school with recognised special educational needs was stated in 2006 by the then Department for Children, Schools and Families (DCSF) to be 2.6 per cent, our finding that nearly 50 per cent of intercountry adopted children are considered by their parents as having special needs was quite astounding and opened our eyes to a significant issue.

Dr Dana Johnson of the University of Minnesota International Adoption Clinic was one of the speakers OASIS brought over to talk about his research. The clinic was set up in 1986 and Dana has been carrying out longitudinal studies on intercountry adoptees ever since. Part of his research has been looking at brain development, and in particular the effects of malnutrition pre and post partum on brain formation. (Full details can be found on www.peds.umn.edu/iac/ and follow the link to research.) In summary, one of the things they found was that in malnourished mothers key chemical elements are not passed on to the foetus and this can inhibit the formation of parts of the brain. This is an area of research that has made huge strides over the past few years and continues to do so.

However, at the time we were first trying to find ways around our children's learning issues, a lot of this information was not out in the public arena, and certainly not part of the general adoption communities' information bank.

We took the children to an educational psychologist to see if there were any particular strategies that we could use. We had tutors to work with them as well as doing our best to help them overcome some of their difficulties. But outside of academic learning school was going really well.

The birth families

At about the same time as the children started primary school, we started the process of trying to reconnect with their birth families in Guatemala. This was obviously a very important decision and not one to be made lightly – some would say it was inappropriate for us to make it and that it should have been made by the children themselves when they were old enough.

We thought long and hard and read a lot about it. We also learned from intercountry adopters and adoptees (mostly from other countries as there are relatively few in the UK). In particular, a group of Latin American adoptees in Canada very generously shared their experiences. Many of the countries in Central and Latin America have the same legal structure, which allows for relinquishment, so their guidance was particularly apt.

The conclusion most of them came to was that it was better to search now rather than wait till the children were

18 or post-adolescent. The reasons were many, but the key ones were that it would be helpful for the children to be able to establish their identities and have a positive view of their origins, that it would eliminate guilt (it wasn't their fault, they did nothing wrong to be given up for adoption), that the children's understanding of their background would be based on reality not fantasy, that waiting increased the chance of failure of the search or the death of key individuals.

One of the other key factors for us was the absence of professionals from the process. The structure in Guatemala simply did not have the budget (or inclination) to provide for any social work intermediaries. However, we had heard through the "Big List", the international e-group for Guatemalan adoptions, about a lady in Guatemala who helped adoptive families re-contact birth families. Her name was "S" and we managed to get in contact with her via email. We gave her all the information we had, and scanned copies of our two birth mothers' identity cards and last known addresses. "S" does not like to go through foster carers or lawyers; this is in order to keep birth families safe, as she can pretend she is representing missionary donors who have selected the families via a church. Even so, we know of birth mothers who have been robbed and murdered very shortly after being contacted by adoptive families, the supposition being that they had been given sums of money or other commodities.

So with a fair amount of trepidation we set "S" to the task of finding our children's birth families. We sent her letters and photos to share with them if we were lucky enough for her to find them. We also knew that at least one of our birth families lived a long, long way away and that not only was there virtually no communication infrastructure, but also that it was not going to be easy for "S" to fit in a search in such a remote region into her schedule.

Nevertheless, after quite a few weeks she contacted us

with some very mixed news. She had been able to establish some contact with members of Veronica's birth family, but they reported that "V" had moved away and did not give any more information, so the trail went cold there. They obviously had no knowledge of the child being born and so "S" judged it too dangerous to continue the investigation lest she reveal information which might endanger the birth mother's concealment.

On the other hand, she had found Ossie's birth mother more or less where we had last known of her. She was very happy to hear from us, was incredibly grateful for the photos and the letter, and looked forward to any further news.

This, at least, was exactly what we had been hoping for, so we continued the communication. Over time it became clear that her whole family were aware of the situation, including her new partner and father of our child's half-brothers, and that she was open to our visiting. It also turned out that she was pregnant and so we were able to help provide some funds for a local doctor so that she would have basic ante-natal care. He checked everything was all right and gave her loads of vitamins and supplements to maximise her health and that of her child.

So we started looking into going back to Guatemala AND visiting birth family. A while back I had been driving Holly van Gulden, the wonderful therapist, and author of *Real Parents, Real Children*, to one of her speaking engagements, and had the opportunity to ask her about the optimum time to take children adopted from overseas back to their country of birth. She said that early visits are fine, but the period when children are likely to gain most, in her opinion, is between eight and adolescence and that multiple visits tend to build on each other.

But she also made it clear that, in her opinion, visits during adolescence in general can be problematic but doing so in the middle phase, when children start to withdraw from their parents (and significantly lower their opinions of them!!) and experience periods of sadness from the psychological loss of that close bond, is putting an unfair burden on adopted children. When this starts varies from child to child but is generally taken to be around the 14/15 age range (with girls usually being ahead of boys).

So we decided that sooner would be better than later (especially if we wanted to have a second visit before that difficult phase), and once again the Guatemalan adoption community were incredibly generous in sharing their experiences of returning to their children's homeland. A few key points of advice were:

- to allow acclimatisation/stabilisation time at the start – not to dive in after long flights
- to ensure we had an appropriate mix of fun and serious activities
- to allow the children to choose which parts of their culture to celebrate
- to go to language school for a while to help the family to integrate
- to leave time around key experiences for the children to process them
- to get everyone to write/record diaries
- to be happy whatever happens

So we started to make our plans to go to Guatemala in the summer of 2006.

Our third trip to Guatemala

I have mentioned before that we had had a number of student/au pairs from Mexico and, in particular, from San Luis Potosi. They were now all friends and had kept in contact with each other, with other Mexican friends they had made in London, and of course with us. Since there were no direct flights to Guatemala City and since we knew it was a very long and wearisome trip, we decided to break our journey in Mexico on the way out and on the way back. In fact (copying the plans of some of our dearest friends) we decided to spend a week in the Yucatan in a tiny beach resort on the way home.

So at the end of July we set off on our long journey – armed to the teeth with books, games and electronic devices! After an overnight stop in Mexico City we set off to meet our friends. It was very noticeable that the children had switched on to the fact that the vast majority of people looked very like them. In addition, they were eating their favourite food (actually preferred to Guatemalan food, because although it uses the same ingredients, Mexican food has a lot more flavour and spice). The breakfast in Mexico City was so good – in particular the *pan dulce* or sweet bread and scrambled eggs with chorizos – that it is used as the standard to measure against in our family to this day.

We drove up to San Miguel de Allende and met up with two of our former au pairs. Detox from the journey included a leisurely visit to the local hot spring resort – so relaxing and yet invigorating. It was great to spend time with them and their husbands and to relax. Best of all it was good for the children to go back over the time we had all spent together, about how much fun and love had been shared and the bonds we all had made. It meant that they were really centred and strong for the next part of our journey.

After a short drive to the airport we flew to Guatemala City. We had arranged to stay overnight at the hotel where we had stayed with them when we first met, and where Ossie and I had waited anxiously for entry clearance. We had the famous burgers for supper and retold the stories of our time there. We all went down for the famous buffet breakfast – and saw all the new adoptive parents with their children: little dark skinned babies in the arms of white parents. To our children it was just very normal – we have so many friends who are in mixed marriages or whose children are transracially adopted that it is nothing out of the ordinary. However, they did comment on some of the parents' attitudes and language. One could not help but overhear some of the conversations about where they had been and what they had seen in Guatemala, and also how they referred to the people and the situation. Guatemala City is certainly a dangerous place and one where precautions should be taken. But some of the parents had virtually walled themselves up in the hotel, and would not venture out, and thus had only very sensationalist understandings of what was happening and of the realities for most Guatemalans. Some of them were afraid to go even to places like Antigua (the old capital), which is a UNESCO heritage site and is kept very, very safe.

We took a little time to visit the British Embassy and to go to the shopping mall where I had bought Ossie's Mickey Mouse boots, before setting off for Antigua. We had decided that to help communication when meeting the birth family and foster family, we would attend a language school and study in the mornings, while leaving the afternoons free. The school was based in the ruins of a monastery that had been destroyed in the huge earthquake of 1773, and had a few *casitas* or bungalows in the gardens. We had rented one of these on the advice of American friends who did so every year. We each had an individual teacher so that we could learn at our own pace and in the way that suited us best – at what seemed to us to be ridiculously cheap prices.

The teachers were fantastic – obviously very experienced and happy to work with us. At the end of the first morning, the children wanted to know if they could carry on in the afternoon! Each teacher had a separate cubicle or area outside in the stunningly beautiful gardens of the monastery, full to bursting with flowers and scents and birds and butterflies. Veronica was very proud of the fact that her teacher commanded a castle – a gazebo on top of a mound.

My teacher was happy to help me prepare for all the questions I wanted to ask and to have ready answers to the questions we felt might be asked of us. We also had long discussions about intercountry adoption from Guatemala, the realities of life for families, the deep-set corruption throughout the state, starting from the very top (all the last five presidents have, on leaving office, been indicted for fraud and theft of millions of dollars). Sometimes some of the other teachers would join us to share their thoughts and opinions.

The teachers were not confined to the school grounds. Since they were with us on a one-to-one basis, they were free to take any of us where we wanted to go and help us to learn whatever areas of language we were most interested in.

The children were taken by their teachers to restaurants and places to play so that they had the opportunity to interact with other Guatemalan children. Even though their Spanish was limited, play is a universal language and they had a good time. Elly went out with her teacher and found all the best shops!

As part of the school curriculum we went on a trip to the Ixel women's weaving co-operative in the village of San Antonio Aguas Calientes. Here they showed us many of the traditional crafts of Guatemala, and explained a lot of the symbolism contained in the weavings. They also showed us how maize is ground and added to slaked lime and ash (masa) and then added to water, rolled into balls flattened between the palms and made into tortillas, which are then cooked on a large iron plate over a fire.

Veronica was asked if she wanted to volunteer to be dressed in *traje* or traditional indigenous clothing, which the women had woven. This consists of a *huipil* or square cut, intricately decorated woven blouse, worn over a *corte* (tube skirt) tied with a woven belt, the *faje*. Two grandmotherly ladies helped her into it and showed her how to adjust it. They then showed her how to grind wheat and coffee on the three-legged *metate*, a square flat shaped pestle and mortar where the pestle is used more like a rolling pin.

We then went into the smoke-filled kitchen tacked on the back of the store where a fire burned between two rocks and watched the tortillas being cooked. They were not hugely appetising and tasted quite ashy and smoky. We were told how most Guatemalan women get up well before dawn (helped by their daughters if they are over six or seven years old) and make hundreds of these palm-sized tortillas for the family for the day. They are sometimes all that the children will eat. Those who work may get some beans as well but meat is eaten very rarely. The choking acrid smoke made the room almost unbearable. Salutary lessons.

Our next big trip was to visit Behrhorst Partners for Development (BPD: www.behrhorst.org), the main UK Guatemalan Families Association charity partner.

BPD started off as a health-based charity that was so successful that its mother and child health programme was taken over by the Guatemalan Government. It has also been used by major international NGOs as a blueprint for successful sustainable development. So now they had moved on in the communities where they are based to support the health programme with complementary public health and development projects, which they describe as a "backpack" of components comprising:

- **Healthy homes**

    access to running water, gray water filters, sanitary latrines, safer stoves, kitchen gardens

- **Strong families**

    fortified meals for chronically malnourished

children, nutrition education for mothers and early childhood education (including building schools)

- **Sustainable communities**

leadership development, allowing community members to advocate effectively on behalf of their communities and micro-loans

It is also really important to emphasise the fact that Behrhorst's goal is:

> *...to work in respectful partnership with Mayan Guatemalans to have a positive impact on the problems associated with Guatemala's history of violence against indigenous populations, natural disasters, poverty, illiteracy and disastrously high rates of infant and maternal death.*

The local area project co-ordinators from BPD came round to our hotel early (before 6am!!) and took us off to San Antonio Choatalun, one of the first villages where Behrhorst put in place their "backpack" of projects. We went in their 4x4 pick-up because ordinary cars cannot get over the tracks that serve as roads up in the "highlands" as the region is known colloquially. The kids got to sit in the truck bed once we got off the highway and into the countryside – one of the highlights of the whole trip for them!

The countryside is very mountainous; the flattest area in the village was the football pitch, which sloped at 35°! The houses are mostly made from wooden sticks with a clay/mud daub forced between them. The better houses have some form of tin roof, mainly made of cut open tin drums. The poorer ones are thatched with palm fronds. In the better houses the kitchen is in an annexe or lean-to, separated from the rest of the accommodation. But in the poorer houses everything is in one room. Some of the houses have a wooden platform to sleep on, but in others everyone sleeps on straw mats on the floor.

Our first port of call was the school that BPD had built – a concrete block building with a tin roof with two school rooms and two separate buildings housing the kitchen and the toilets. We sat down at American-style combined desks and chairs (a very tight fit for adults, especially larger Western ones!). We saw how lessons were taught in the local indigenous language as well as Spanish, and how the curriculum contained really practical elements, such as trying to introduce more efficacious crops and agricultural methods.

In the village it was immediately very clear how successful the project had been and continued to be. We were introduced to a girl called Maria and her family. She was eight and very shy. Bearing in mind that Guatemala has the world's second highest rate of stunted growth (after Bangladesh), it was noticeable that she was already as tall as her mother, nearly as tall as her father, and appeared well nourished and healthy. In addition, she went to school every day. Two-and-a-half years after BPD started their work in this village, the results for this girl and others have been dramatic.

The key elements of change – healthy homes, strong families and sustainable communities – were all clearly visible.

Before the water project there was no water in the village – and certainly nothing drinkable. So all the women (including pregnant ones) and children had to spend an average of one to three hours per day just to carry water to their homes for basic cooking and hygiene needs. This easily translates into eight hours per day per family, a huge expenditure of time. And to make it worse the lack of sufficient quantities of clean water contributed to many diseases, adding to the vicious cycle of poverty and deprivation.

A fundamental principle of the way BPD works is that

the village community has to really own a project. All the families have to sign up to it before it can start. Then they have to contribute to it. The hard work here has been done by the villagers themselves, including children, women and men. Each family contributed 42 workdays, members of the community collected and split wood, and each family gave $20 to pay for sawing the planks used in constructing the tank.

Now each family has a *pila* (a double sink and washboard combination) and tap with clean running water to prepare food and cook as well as to wash their clothes and themselves. They have invested almost $500 in cash and/or labour, and this in an area where the average daily wage is under $4. This is a very efficient and just method, which ensures that not one cent of the funding gets lost to the corruption so rampant in most public projects. And it is simple and efficient to administer.

But running water also creates waste water, so BPD built into the backpack a very simple system of volcanic sand-based filters. The water can then be used for the kitchen gardens, situated just down hill. BPD teaches the women to grow vegetables, fruit trees and protein-rich grains such as amaranth, which all greatly improve families' nutritional intake.

The other use for the waste water is in the amazing cast concrete toilets that BPD helps communities to make on site and install. Obviously these are a huge health benefit compared with previous alternatives: a bucket to be emptied out somewhere in the woods or fields or open pits. But there is a problem about what to do with the end product, so to speak.

The solution? So simple it strikes me as brilliant – filter beds again to purify the water, and avocado and banana trees to absorb as much of the nutrients and moisture as possible. End result – loads of the easiest "ready packaged" fruit to feed the children.

Another keystone of the backpack project are the stoves. Quite simply the stoves reduce by about 70 per cent + the amount of firewood consumed by a family and eliminate 99 per cent of the smoke. (You will recall how badly the smoke from the fire affected us when we visited the weavers' co-operative.) Now, whilst this has obvious benefits, it is the more subtle changes that make the difference. Without a stove it takes five days' pay to buy the family's firewood for a month – with one, it takes less than the pay for a day-and-a-half.

In Guatemala, thousands of children die before the age of five and the leading cause of death is acute respiratory infection (World Health Organisation). Open cooking fires are responsible for respiratory disease – it has been estimated that the effects on the average Guatemalan woman of cooking over an open fire is the equivalent of smoking two packs of cigarettes every day. And from the day they are born, the children are carried on their mothers' backs while they cook over the open fires. Every year, hundreds of women and children are badly burned when clothing or hair sets on fire or children fall into the burning wood.

So the introduction of stoves is clearly a good idea!

When we went into Maria's family house we were really impressed with the simplicity of the technology that is making such huge changes. Basically the stoves are cast chambers standing on blocks. The lower chamber is the firebox and the top chamber is filled with pumice. Above it is a *plancha* or hotplate made of concentric metal rings. By removing just enough rings to match the pan, energy is transferred directly to the pot, leaving only enough heat in the exhaust gases to provide a draft up the chimney.

Equally important to the health benefits of the stoves is the fact that they free up time and money so that more families can send their children to school – and ultimately education is the best weapon to break the cycle of poverty.

There is an old adage, you need money to make money – and this is proven by BPD's micro-loan scheme. This provides families with funds to buy livestock, which can be fed in part on the scraps and peelings from the kitchen garden, and then sold as meat to pay off the loan and make a profit. In addition, the less marketable cuts of the meat contribute positively to the family's diet. Alternatively, micro-loans are available to start other businesses – including weaving and making products to sell to tourists (us!).

As we walked about the village, we were left with the overwhelming impression that the whole community had the confidence to take itself forward through its own efforts – not relying on charity from outside. It felt great that we, as a part of the GFA, had been able to help. It was also an incredible feeling to be welcomed as part of their community – and I think the children in particular felt this very deeply. It gave them real insight into the society they had been born into – the strength of traditions and the gradual inclusion of modern additions through the respectful work of BPD. But most of all we were moved by the brightness in the children's eyes and their knowledge that they have real hope for a successful future.

A few days later we had another unbelievably early start as we finally headed off for our meeting with Ossie's birth family.

The days before had been filled with a quiet anticipation – probably more for Elly and me than the children. For us, at least, there was no fear or sense of competition. There was concern about how everyone was going to cope with their emotions. We had no idea how positive or negative it was going to be for either of the children, the one being reminded of her lack of contact or the one who, for the first time in six-and-a-half years, was going to have contact with his birth family – and indeed meet some of them for the first time.

So at five o'clock in the morning four somnambulists got into a big white people carrier and set off from Antigua towards Chiquimula and the Honduran border. We stopped on the way for breakfast where an outcrop of obsidian had been cut through by the creation of the road, and collected a piece to take home. Discussions of how the Maya had been able to use obsidian as their primary material for domestic and warlike purposes alike took up most of the rest of the journey, and time passed quickly until, almost without being ready for it, we were at the centre of the town of Chiquimula, "*la Perla del Oriente*", some 100 miles from Guatemala City.

We were due to meet at the Central Park so we parked the car and found somewhere to sit and wait. It was Sunday and the benches and walkways were crowded with families representing all generations – from tiny babies to wizened and grizzled elders – maybe grandparents or even great-grandparents. The appointed time for us to meet came and went – Central American timekeeping, or had they changed their minds? Then just as "S" was starting to look a bit anxious, there was "M", Ossie's birth mother, looking a bit panicked – the middle one of Ossie's half-brothers had got lost in the crowd. A search party was quickly convened and a few minutes later we were all reunited.

That broke the ice and removed all the obstacles of shyness and hesitation, and made it so much easier to just sit down again and start talking. There was so much we had felt we needed to say, but a lot did not need to be spoken. Elly and "M" just sat and hugged for ages, two mothers who shared their love for a beautiful boy. Ossie (like most boys) was more hesitant with adults so was a bit shy when greeting and embracing "M", but showed no such uncertainty with his (half) brothers. In seconds he was running around with the older two, some two and four years younger than him.

"M" then showed her incredible generosity and understanding by greeting and hugging Veronica as part of her family, as Ossie's sister. That gesture alone probably made the whole trip worthwhile for Veronica, and gave her a little of what she had been looking for – although her lack of contact with their own birth family was hurting and still continues to do so.

It was then announced that the rest of the family were waiting for us at the local Pollo Campero (fried chicken restaurant). So we agreed we would have another quiet time together later and we set off to have lunch.

When we entered there was a large group waiting for us: grandparents, uncles, aunts and a variety of cousins, about thirteen or fourteen people in all. Some of his uncles and aunts were younger than Ossie as his grandmother's youngest child was only two! We ordered loads of food and sat down to what felt like a party, a celebration of a family reunion. "S" was busy translating and explaining. Lots of things came easily, but one was also brought up short by other levels of understanding and misunderstanding. For example, how far away places are and the concept of "overseas". They could understand distances as far as Guatemala City. They had seen airplanes flying overhead. They knew there had once been a train system through their area (indeed they lived on part of the disused railway bed). They understood the idea of borders – Honduras being only 20 miles or so away. But it was far outside the realms of their understanding to really comprehend where we lived, and what that meant in terms of travel.

We had brought with us a beach ball with a map of the world and "M"'s sister, who was the only one who could read, could identify Guatemala. We then showed her where England and London were and the United States. The huge spaces of the oceans were unfathomable, although some of them had seen the sea.

Another, and more successful, ice-breaker was a paper

fortune teller (made from a sheet of paper folded into squares and triangles, that you can tuck your fingers in to manipulate). Elly helped the children to adorn each section with simple (and polite!) Spanish phrases, numbers and colours. Veronica was able to go round the table and play the game with everyone, old and young, and a crowd of children in tow, laughing at each of the victims in turn. I had a conversation with Ossie's grandfather and we talked about how I had promised to bring him back and we had done so. I asked how the family were doing and how they felt about the adoption and Ossie now some seven or so years later.

With "S"'s help, he explained his cultural view of family. The term *familia* in Guatemala usually goes far beyond the nuclear family. The Mayan "family unit" includes not only parents and children but also extended family. The Mayan household is typically augmented by the presence of a grandparent, an aunt or uncle, or a daughter, abandoned by her partner, with children of her own, and frequently by an orphaned relative, a poor godchild, or a child from the community in need of a family. Land shortages mean newly married couples frequently take up residence in the home of one of the parental families. In addition, a large number of children helps the *familia* meet their everyday labour needs and provides security in old age. And the *familia* includes members not affiliated by blood.

The term *compadre* is often used for a best friend, companion or comrade, but it actually means co-parent, a role latterly taken over by the Christian religion and transformed into the godparent. In Mayan society it is not unusual for aunts and uncles, grandparents, godparents or non-blood-related friends to be the primary care providers for children, and the *familia* relies on all extended members for financial assistance, advice and emotional support.

Thus, Ossie's grandfather explained, by giving us one of their children we had become their *compadres* and all of both Elly's and my families were inextricably tied to his.

I said that it was indeed an honour for him to allow us into his *familia* and we very much appreciated the privilege. We once again confirmed our promises to care for Ossie and bring him up to respect his family, its culture and traditions.

We also had the opportunity to talk at greater length to "M" and to understand the pressures on her and her household. Her new partner, and father of Ossie's half-brothers, was unable to be there as he was a truck driver who worked a long way from home and was sometimes absent for weeks at a time. He was fully aware of Ossie's existence and was happy that we were caring for him.

"M"'s biggest problem was that she was sharing a house with her new partner's parents and other family members, and she very much wanted to build on a lean-to, to give herself and her children a bit more privacy and space. We agreed to consider helping her with this.

We then asked about education as the older boys were just getting to the age when they should be attending primary school regularly. We had a long discussion about whether "M" would be happy for us to sponsor all the boys through school, and how this might improve their long-term prospects.

After lunch we left with "M" and the boys to have a little bit more private time. Ossie opened up a lot and was clearly enjoying time with his half-brothers. He still did not have a lot to say to "M" but was comfortable in her presence and happy to share touches and looks that communicated all that each needed to know.

We had brought some presents for the boys – England football shirts and trackies in England backpacks and a football each. For "M" a photo album with photos of Ossie over the years as well as copies of the ones we took at the British Embassy interview all those years before. What can you give the woman who has given you her greatest prize, her firstborn, to care for? We tried to ensure that she could see the love we have for him and that we truly do believe that we are all part of one large *familia*, separated by many miles but joined in our shared love.

The time came for us to part and we watched through tear-brimmed eyes as "M" and her boys walked away through the scrub and trees, England backpacks hitched up high and proud. We had had a family hug, supporting each other silently. It was a while before we could move – everyone full of their own thoughts and emotions. We got back in the car and set off back to Antigua.

As we drove on through the cooling Guatemalan afternoon we all talked and reflected on the day's events. "S", who has been through this many times with many families, felt that this had really been a very special day, and that "M" and her family – *our* family – are truly a treasure. Slowly we came down from the emotional high plateau we had unknowingly been on all day and breathed less rarefied air. We were able to laugh and cry at our shared memories of the reunion. And then, as a most appropriate conclusion to a day like that, we met a huge, incredibly dramatic and spectacular thunderstorm...and got a puncture! Our lovely driver had had a heart operation some years before so, still dressed in my best, I changed the tyre to the evident amusement of our children and all the locals.

When we drove through the town "S" pointed out the road Veronica's birth mother used to live in before she moved. It was a crisis point for Veronica who, whilst strengthened by "M"'s open-hearted inclusion of her in the *familia*, was still desperately hurt by the fact that she did not have links with her own birth family, that she had not been reunited, that she still felt that huge loss. We hugged and kissed her but knew we could never fill that empty space. It is terrible to feel so helpless in the face of your child's pain – but that is also part and parcel of being an adoptive parent. We got back to the hotel late that night and all collapsed into bed immediately after supper, completely exhausted. The next day would most definitely be a rest day!

We had one more goal to achieve before we left Guatemala and that was to meet up with the fantastic foster family that had cared for Ossie and Veronica for so long, whilst all the delays had extended the process. We had been in contact with Silvia and her husband on their mobile and they wanted to pick us up and take us to their house. We had not been able to visit them while they were fostering, as this was seen to be inappropriate and dangerous at the time. However, they felt it was fine now, and they wanted us to see their home.

So on yet another beautiful sunny day we jumped into their car and set out for Mixco, Guatemala's third largest city and effectively a suburb of Guatemala City. Their house is a jumble of rooms and apartments for all the families that make up their *familia*. Silvia and her husband and son live on the ground floor next to the enclosed double garage. Her siblings and their families occupy the middle floor and her mother lives on the top floor. All the family members are foster carers. As we sat and talked with them they told us more of their family story.

Silvia's mother had become a foster carer after her husband left when her own children were growing up, so it had seemed totally natural for the children and their spouses to follow in her footsteps. Everyone remembered Ossie and Veronica and were really happy to see them again – apparently not many families had stayed in contact and even fewer visited. It turned out that Veronica had been a special favourite of Silvia's mother because she had been so weak and malnourished when she arrived, and she had slept on Granny's pillow and in her bed almost all the time she had been there.

We also met a lot of the children in the house – some the

families' own birth children and some not. There was one little boy who had been matched with adopters, but when the couple had met him and saw that he had the faintest scar from a hare lip, had changed their minds. So Silvia's family just decided to keep him as one of their own – which he clearly was. There was another child with obvious special educational needs whom they cared for during the day so that his mother could go out to work. Silvia's husband worked with a charity dealing with street children, and he had brought a young girl to live with them who was heavily pregnant and whose parents had thrown her out of the family home.

We sat and talked – Ossie ran around with the boys, Veronica cuddling up with Granny, of whom she seemed to have some deep seated pre-verbal memories. Granny ran her hand soothingly over Veronica's hair and she just melded into her. We talked about their memories of Ossie and Veronica, of how we had spent time together with Silvia and the invaluable lessons she had taught us, of how we had felt when I came to take Ossie home, and how afraid I had been. We talked about what was happening in Guatemalan adoptions and how they would cope if Guatemala closed its doors to foreign adopters, as seemed likely (and actually happened some six months later). We told them all about the children's lives in England, about how their early time had affected them but also how the obvious bonds they had made to each other and to Silvia and her family had enabled us to build our family attachments so securely. We tried to express our gratefulness for all the work they had done, but they dismissed it as work; they said it had been a blessing.

After a huge and very delicious meal, for which all the children sat at the table in a real party atmosphere, we returned to our hotel. Once again we reflected on the difference between our developed nation's "nuclear family" lifestyle and culture and the open supportive developing nation's *familia*, which had embraced us. It really made me think about what we have lost in our movement forward through prosperity and material security.

A few days later we flew to Mexico to stay in a beach house just a few miles from Tulum. Our bungalow was right on the beach, about 100 metres of pure white sand away from the clear blue sea. It was basic but perfect for what we needed. The veranda had places to hang hammocks and we had a palm tree right outside. It was the turtle egg laying season, so the lights went out really early – about eight or nine o'clock so as not to disturb or disorient them (apparently they need to use reflections on the sea to find their way back).

The second night we were there, we were called by locals to see a giant sea turtle digging this huge pit and laying eggs in it. We were all completely fascinated and amazed. A man from the conservation agency came, driving down the beach on his quad bike and collected about half of the eggs and sealed them up in a box to take back to the centre. This was to ensure the greatest number possible survived by offering perfect conditions and protection against collectors. At the end we followed the turtle as she made her weary way back to the sea, and the man from the conservation agency said it was OK to touch the turtle gently just before she went into the waves, so both Ossie and Veronica got to do so. What a thrill!!

The next day, having spent it building huge turtles out of sand, we had a turtle come right outside our little house and lay eggs under our palm tree. Unbelievable.

We spent our few days on the beach relaxing and having fun, swimming and making sand castles – we developed a fine line in Mayan pyramids – and most of all just being together. Allowing all of our memories to wash through and working out what we had learned was very beneficial to all of us.

For the final part of our travels we set off to see some

of the fantastic Mayan sites in this part of Mexico. Probably the most famous of these is *Chichen Itza,* or Chicken Pizza as the kids renamed it. It is a magnificent place with huge stone buildings and temples, fantastic carvings recording the lives of the rulers and key events, evidence of the incredible astronomical and mathematical sophistication of these distant ancestors of our children. However, the children were most interested in the Ball Court where an ancient game, whose rules are lost in time, was played with one side (it is hard to tell from the carvings whether it is the winners or the losers) sacrificed to the Gods as the conclusion to the game – no chance of developing a league then. The frieze of skulls surrounding the area was particularly attractive to our two...shades of styles to come!

We also visited the newly discovered *Ek Balam* where many of the original wall paintings and decorations are still visible, giving a brilliant impression of how startling and colourful these places must have been in their glory. Even now the huge stone masses and buildings are awe inspiring, but when one imagines them covered in brightly, almost garishly painted plaster then the image is mind blowing.

Finally, we flew via Mexico City back home to England – to fill the hall with our bags, stagger into the kitchen for that first cup of English tea and a return to our usual family life.

But we were changed, in many ways and at many levels, and it would take time for this to be assimilated. For me the greatest impact had been the understanding I had been given about *familia* and community – about being a *compadre*. There are lots of scholarly works about social structures in Central America. Researchers have looked at all the members of extended families and the roles they are expected to play. But it is another thing altogether to see it and feel it. I have taken great strength from it and it informs a lot of my decisions and the efforts I put into the intercountry and domestic adoption communities.

At the end of the holiday the children and Elly went back to school and I went back to work. It is important to acknowledge that our children's lives are just "normal" for 99 per cent of the time. They go to school, they play sports or music, they have sleepovers or go to parties and get into trouble in exactly the same way as all their friends, however their families may have been formed.

Moving and changes

The next major event in our lives was when we moved house. Although the children had been involved in the process throughout – choosing the house, who would have which room, how they would have to go to school and come home by train every day – it was more emotionally upsetting for them than we had expected.

We had done quite a lot of travelling, and in a way the children had found a second home in Croatia because everything was very familiar there, and they returned to the same places every time. But our home was a more important part of their sense of security than we had anticipated.

We moved immediately after our summer holiday in Croatia, so I suppose there was also the added pressure of a new school year and new form teacher. It also did not help that at the time we had our least open and supportive au pair, who wasn't as good as her predecessors or successor at enthusing and motivating Ossie and Veronica. Lovely girl, but she just could not impart that spark of passion and excitement.

We tried to make things as personalised as possible as quickly as we could, but even now, more than four years later, the children have a deep nostalgia for their old house. On reflection we could have done things better.

I think the key that we missed was spending enough time preparing Ossie and Veronica and encouraging them to voice their thoughts and fears about the move, which raised insecurities in the children that we had not foreseen.

I suspect that we portrayed it only as a positive change (which I suppose is how Elly and I saw it) – when obviously for them it had a more powerful resonance of loss. We did not spend enough time talking about this element of their experience, both before and immediately afterwards. We did try to explain what the changes would be like and had done things like dry runs of their trips to school. But we had not done enough. We should have taken photos of the old house and of their rooms, or perhaps, even better, let them have a disposable camera to take their own photos. We had packers to help us get things into boxes, and I think we should have allowed the children to be more involved. We resumed routines as quickly as possible, but we did not acknowledge the break to routine and the time that had been lost.

The children did get over the move after a short while, although they sometimes say they wish we were still in our old house. Moving had never been mentioned to us as an area of potential disquiet for adopted children, but now we have been able to share our experience with other adopters, and they have told us that they have benefited from greater awareness.

As time went on we did quite a lot of work on the house. This enabled us to "personalise" it more: the children could get involved in making decisions about their own rooms as well as other parts of the house. This gave them more sense of control and ownership and they are now almost as attached to this house as they were to the old one.

Life carried on in our new house. The biggest change to our daily routine was the amount of travel the children had to do. They were still at the same school – we had decided that it was not an option to change – and so still had the same circle of friends. But they now went to and from school by train. They went to school by themselves as there were quite a number of others who travelled the same way.

One morning, one of our nephews from Japan was visiting and stayed overnight. He went off with the children on the train in the morning and was chatting away to them and also took some photos on his phone. One of the regular travellers who knew them (they tended to sit in the same area in the same carriage on the same train every day) took the time to phone the school to ask them to inform us that a stranger had been taking photos of Ossie and Veronica. It restored our faith in human nature a bit as well as making us feel that the children were safe on the train.

The next big challenge to come along was SATS and the move to secondary school. I think sometimes we adults can forget that things that we feel are insignificant compared to our problems of work, relationships and paying the mortgage, to the child can seem insuperable. The idea of SATS was very scary and even worse was the move from primary school to secondary school.

At primary school, essentially the same group of twenty to thirty children spend all day with the same teacher and build very strong relationships with their teacher and each other. They can feel very secure. Secondary school is presented as "big school" where one is expected to be more independent in a much bigger environment with many more students, with different teachers and classes for each subject.

And on top of all that, there is the school play or musical or whatever at the end of primary school, in which it seems all year six students are expected to perform in public – virtual torture for anyone who is shy.

Ossie was first up to meet this challenge. His class had always been really tight – boys and girls together were a great team. Ossie had overcome a lot of his reading difficulties and become an interested reader. The key had actually been "Top Trumps", the card game where you choose a different category to compete with your opposition. Being able to read quickly is necessary – and Ossie being as competitive as he is, found his motivation. It still took him time to be a fluent reader but he was on the way.

Regrettably, like so many primary schools, Ossie's school concentrated on teaching the children to pass SATS. One has to acknowledge that they did so successfully, and Ossie ended up with quite satisfactory scores, but I felt that a year had been lost to learning test techniques, rather than gaining knowledge, a love of learning and the ability to learn by yourself.

The summer ended and Ossie started in secondary school. Care had been taken to keep children together with friends from primary school so he could immediately see some familiar faces. Nevertheless, it was quite hard for him to get into the steeply increased level of personal responsibility. I think he also found the level of anonymity hard. Rather than being a well known (and hopefully liked) character in the small context of primary school with some 150 pupils in total, he was an unknown in the sea of faces of the 180+ children in his year who swiftly merged with other years.

But this did allow Ossie to control information about his background. His friends from primary knew he was adopted, but it took him nearly a year before he wanted any of his new friends to know, and then he chose to share it with only two of them.

Nearly all adopted children and their parents get asked adoption-related questions often based on misinformation. Sometimes they can be intrusive and hurtful, although usually this is through ignorance and clumsiness not hostility. But parents, and more importantly children, need to find a way to deal with such questions, and also, within themselves, to cope with the feelings these questions arouse.

Since adoption is not generally part of normal family

conversations, children very often have confused ideas about adoption – gleaned from the media, films, stories, books and other children. These questions can be as extreme as:

'Are babies sold on the internet?'

'Are babies stolen from their parents and adopted?'

'Did your real mother not like you?'

All of these questions have been asked of our children.

The motivations behind the questions range from simple curiosity and a desire to learn more, to fear that it might happen to them. So non-adoptees may ask in a spirit of openness or with a view to emphasising difference. Also, because they almost instinctively know this is private and problematic territory, they will ask the questions when a child is at their most vulnerable, when adults are not around.

So it is important that parents find a way to help their children prepare for these questions and to come up with answers that they are comfortable with and which achieve their desired objectives.

A while ago, OASIS had the team from the Centre for Adoption Support and Education (CASE) in the US come over and run a series of training sessions for children on their WISE Up programme. The WISE Up programme and Powerbook are a very useful means to help adopted children to understand that they are the real experts about adoption. They do not have to give in to anyone else's views. They also learn to make up their minds about the motivations of the person asking the question and what they feel about them. Then they look at the context of the question, is it in public or private, are they alone or with friends, does it follow from the previous conversation or come out of the blue? They are encouraged to think about how they feel about the question.

Lastly, the children learn that they have four simple options as to how they respond:

Walk away – stay silent, ignore what has been said and walk away

It's private – this is appropriate to say to anyone. It's your story – you decide

Share something – think carefully about sharing some of your story

Educate – talk about adoption in general, not your story

With only a little practice children are able to take these strategies on board and use them, and as they do, they learn how empowering being able to control such situations can be.

Our children also learned one other really important technique, which is simply to ask: 'why are you asking?' Sometimes you find a link to adoption, sometimes you find out about a genuine wish to learn and know, and sometimes it forces people to question their own behaviour.

So Ossie was able to use the techniques he had learned and practised to control who had what information, and to cope with the flood of questions thrown at him in his first days of secondary school.

Since his school is a specialist sports school, Ossie found the general standard of physical abilities higher than in primary, which, allied with the much larger numbers of pupils, meant for the first time he had to work to get into the first team! This was really good for him and he rose to the challenge. It made him focus on what sports he really wanted to excel at. So football and cricket were sidelined and rugby, tennis and table tennis came to the fore. Even so, his willingness to give most things a try and his natural abilities meant he would be called on at the last minute, if a team was short of a player, to take part in sports he knew little or nothing about, and sometimes even to represent the school in them.

Veronica faced the same challenges a year later. Her

special educational needs are more severe and she finds exams and tests even more frustrating. Thanks to a lot of work by the primary school and ourselves, we had managed to get Veronica readers for many of her SATS, so that she had finally been able to understand the questions. With readers in place, her results were really satisfying and helped build her self-esteem in preparation for secondary school. In the school play she was "Fingers", a pickpocket, part of the Artful Dodger's gang, and seemed to have no problems at all in being a credible criminal!

Again, the first few weeks at school were very tough as she became accustomed to the self-discipline of organising herself in the much larger environment. Her best friend at school is a girl, also adopted (but domestically). We had met her adoptive parents at a support group when they were considering intercountry adoption, but the local authority had offered them domestic adoption and they had adopted two siblings. We had become friends and stayed in contact with them for quite a number of years, but we hadn't seen them for some while when we met them again at the parents' open evening. The girls straight away resumed their friendship and it endures to this day.

It was very interesting to note that both Veronica and "A", her best friend, were much more up front about being adopted and shared the information with staff and pupils. They use it as their "specialist subject" in a lot of the projects in physical and social health, religious education and English – they have decided to follow the "education" option of the WISE Up programme as much as they can.

This means that their school friends and colleagues are much more aware of the issues in adoption – but it also opens them up to more questions. By being very open we have always been able to talk to Veronica about how she feels and what she wants to say. We can therefore work together to help her practise ways of expressing herself and giving the information she wants – but also keeping private those parts she does not wish to share.

As an extension of this, Veronica has also been much more willing to take part in the media work we have done. In fact, she fronted up for the family on the Channel 4 programme *4thought* (www.channel4.com/programmes/4thoughttv/episode-guide/series-1/episode-190).

We all thought she did a fantastic job. And it was a useful experience as we were able to exchange views with other contributors.

Racism

One of the areas we talked about was racism.

I sometimes hear parents talk about racism being eliminated in our society. As a white man I cannot presume to talk for people from minority ethnic backgrounds, but to me that simply sounds as if people have yet to confront their prejudices based on "race", ethnicity and class.

Most white communities are reluctant to talk about race and privilege – and British reticence makes it seem even harder for us to do so. But it is a process we need to be able to go through to gain a real understanding of how we interact with society as a whole and to develop a more complete knowledge of ourselves and of others, so that we can relate to the uniqueness of each individual without denying them the influence of the group of which they are a member.

For transracial adoption by white parents to be successful, I believe those parents need to be able to develop awareness of the racism their children will undoubtedly encounter, and move from parenting a child of different heritage to being members of a multi-racial family. This move is not automatic, or indeed trouble-free. You have to do a lot of work to examine your own racial and cultural identity, to confront racism in society and to stretch your inner boundaries in the hope that you will be rewarded by seeing your children develop into adulthood with a strong positive sense of themselves and their family.

Our children to date have not really experienced a lot of racism – partly because they do not visibly belong to a common UK minority ethnic group. However, they are clearly not white British, and identify themselves as Guatemalan British. They have met with some racism in other countries. In the US, Central Americans are a very known and visible minority group – and the same is true to a lesser extent in Spain. But the most notable occasion was when we went to visit Elly's sister in Japan.

A visit to Japan

I had lived in Japan for a couple of years in the late eighties, when it was still a much more closed society and "*gaijin*" were few and far between outside of Tokyo. Things have definitely changed since then, especially among the younger generations, and whilst Japan still sees itself as a homogeneous society, attitudes to foreigners have changed a great deal – but in more rural communities and also among the older generations many of the old attitudes of superiority and exclusiveness persist. *Gaijin* means outsider and many feel it has negative or pejorative connotations, so increasingly it is being replaced by *gaikokujin* – foreign country person.

Most of the time something that may seem racist in Japan comes from the fact that Japanese people are afraid of confrontation and the humiliation (loss of face) of being put in a situation where they cannot do what they perceive to be the right thing. But there is still genuine racism. Some of it is official. In January 2005, Japan's Supreme Court ruled that public employers can refuse to give senior posts to ethnic minorities, even second-generation South Koreans living in Japan, on the basis that foreigners do not have the right to hold positions of authority over ethnic Japanese.

Sometimes it is seeing people recoil slightly from you as

you walk down the street or refusing to give you one of the freebies they are handing out to everyone else on the street. Sometimes it is people leaving seats empty on either side of you on crowded trains and buses. Sometimes it is people trying uncomfortably to avoid eye contact, or staring at you openly as if you were the first white person they had ever seen. Sometimes it is the generalisations like 'that's how *gaijin* think' or as they lean across the table or bar to offer you some morsel: 'Try this. Foreigners can't eat it, you know'. Minor discomforts compared with the violent racism in our own culture's history, but noticeable nonetheless.

So when we went to Japan I had warned the children that sometimes we might be looked at differently and get strange reactions. Elly's sister lives next to the sea in a small community on Sendai Bay (exactly where the tsunami hit the coast in 2011). The community includes a group of houses, a sort of retreat for foreigners established by missionaries over a hundred years ago. Consequently, in the local area, *gaikokujin* are a mundane common sight and attract no attention at all.

We went to Nikko to visit the UNESCO world heritage site incorporating the Toshogu, Futarasan and Rinno-ji shrines, the mausoleum of Tokugawa Ieyasu (on whom the "Shogun" of the book and file are based), the Cedar Avenue and nearby Lake Chuzenji and Kegon waterfall. Because these were places I had visited frequently while I lived in Japan, and because I wanted the children to be able to experience some very typical Japanese things, we stayed in a *minshuku* (a traditional Japanese-style family-owned hotel with its own hot spring baths).

Despite the fact that this is one of the most visited tourist areas in Japan, as soon as we got off the standard tourist trail we ran into all the things I had warned the children about. In the *minshuku* this was genuinely because they were concerned we would not enjoy the experience –

we would not be able to sleep on futons on the floor, we would not be able to cope with the Japanese bath system (we would wash in the water only meant for soaking, the water would be too hot, etc.) let alone the toilets. In other places it was less benign. It gave us an insight into some of the more subtle, non-verbal forms of prejudice and made us think of our own behaviour. Were we exploiting or abusing our status as visitors in a country whose history and culture were so different from ours?

Japan came very much to our minds again in March 2011 when the earthquake and tsunami struck. Wendy, Elly's sister, was fortunate that her house is on top of a cliff overlooking the sea. The earthquake forced her outside where she clung on to a tree, unable to stay on her feet. Minutes later the tsunami warning sounded and she watched as the sea was drawn back almost to the horizon before returning with the 17 metre tall tsunami. Elsewhere it was over 40 metres tall. Nearly 16,000 people died.

Luckily Wendy and her neighbours were able to contact the outside world so we knew she was OK. But she had been due to come with us to Guatemala a few weeks later at Easter – for obvious reasons that part of the plan had to be changed!

Guatemala again

In April 2011, five years since our last visit, we packed our bags once more and set off for Guatemala. We had arranged to meet two of our Latin American friends and had rented a house in Antigua for two weeks.

We had chosen Easter this time because of the famous Holy Week (*Semana Santa*) festivities and processions in Antigua. We planned to visit Ossie's birth family, see Copan, the famous Mayan ruins, and also both of the GFA's charity partners, Behrhorst and Pueblo a Pueblo.

Semana Santa is one of the most spectacular events in all of the Americas, a giant work of community art to which thousands of people in Antigua and nearby towns contribute. Each church has its own *andas* – huge wooden platforms weighing several tons with tableaux of religious figures related to the story of the crucifixion and decorated with flowers and, in the evening, processions and lights! The organisation for each church's processions (because there will be at least one *anda* for the men and another for the women) has been done by each *anda's hermandad*. These can be men's or women's organisations (literally brotherhoods) who co-ordinate the processions. They begin their preparations a full year in advance, making all the arrangements for the music, decorating the *andas* and marshalling the hordes of *cucuruchos* (the penitants who carry the *andas*). There are up to sixty shifts of *cucuruchos* and between eighty and one hundred and twenty *cucuruchos* (matched by height) per *anda*. Each of them pays about ten dollars for the privilege, and senior members of the *hermandad* will contribute much, much more.

Residents along the route invite their *familia* to help them make elaborate, beautiful *alfombras* (carpets of dyed sawdust, flowers and vegetables) during the hours before the procession. Sawdust dyed in vivid colours is used to make bold designs reflecting biblical and Mayan symbols and the whole is then decorated with flowers, native plants and pine needles.

The construction is timed so that the carpets are finished just before the carriers of the float arrive so it looks its best – and then the procession with the *cucuruchos* and the *anda* and accompanying brass band and dignitaries walk over it, and the whole is destroyed – but it is seen as a way to honour Christ's sacrifice and pay penance. If more than one procession goes down a street, a new *alfombra* is made for each procession.

Each procession leaves from its church and follows a route through the streets of Antigua before returning to the church several hours later. The procession is preceded by incense burners, which fill the air with smoke – sometimes so thick that you can barely see. A block behind the main float, the women carry a smaller float (size is relative here) with the figure of the Virgin Mary. Each *anda* has its own brass band, but we did notice that their repertoire was strictly limited and very funereal. There are also men with special poles to lift the electricity and phone cables out of the way. The processions can last for twelve hours or more and sometimes go on throughout the night. The religious rituals are an intriguing mix of the mystical and the traditional blended with the indigenous.

We were overwhelmed by the sense of occasion as we waited for the first procession to come though the cathedral square. Guatemala is a deeply religious country – split equally between Catholics and Evangelicals, and literally hundreds of thousands of locals come out to see and join in the solemn activities. Young and old turn out and it is very evident that this is a genuine part of their culture. We were all moved by the depth of the faith of so many people.

However, I should also note that there are only so many processions most people can take in a week, and the children especially became "burnt out" after a few. But Antigua has many other sights and experiences to offer and we had a lot more on our agenda.

We had arranged once more to visit the Pueblo a Pueblo programme manager in Santiago Atitlan and booked ourselves onto a bus to Panajachel. Since we had been before, we were aware of the way in which one wanders around looking a bit lost until a tout comes up to you to organise a boat to get across the lake. Sure enough the plan worked perfectly and we were soon speeding across Lake Atitlan.

In his 1934 travel book, *Beyond the Mexique Bay*, Aldous Huxley compared Guatemala's Lake Atitlan to Italy's Lake Como. The Italian body of water, he wrote, 'touches the limit of the permissibly picturesque'. Atitlan, however, 'is Como with the additional embellishment of several immense volcanoes. It is really too much of a good thing.' It would be wrong to disagree!

Racing across the deep slate blue water with the sun doing its best to shine through dark stormy clouds it is, one must acknowledge, an indescribably dramatic and beautiful place. But it is also a place that shelters a broad spectrum of activities. Santiago is a centre for art – with a large number of painters, some of whom produce lots of very similar work for the tourist market, but others have developed their own style and techniques. It is also famous as a place of worship and the centre for the country's 100,000 Tzutujil people. In October 2005 during Hurricane Stan it was devastated by massive mudslides, which killed hundreds of the local inhabitants and destroyed much of the infrastructure – including schools and the local (newly completed) hospital which Pueblo a Pueblo had helped to refurbish. Mudslides buried the hospital right up to the roof and destroyed the primary school and many homes and killed over 400 people.

Pueblo a Pueblo worked to restore the hospital and now focuses on a number of long-term solutions supporting child education and family health. One of the projects we went to see was a programme to help children grow their own vegetables – improving their diets now, as well as giving them skills for the future.

We met the Pueblo a Pueblo programme manager Jen Smith in the main square and went off to see the children growing vegetables. The children were obviously having fun working with their teacher. They prepared the soil and planted the seeds directly into shallow trenches. Elsewhere, crops of vegetables were thriving and being watered by hand by other children. Some of the crops were ready to be harvested and we talked to the children about how it felt to eat crops they had helped to grow. The teacher told us about how much difference it was making to the children to be able to eat so much more healthily.

About half of the children in Guatemala are chronically malnourished – and among the indigenous population that can increase to 80 per cent. Overall Guatemala has the fourth worst performance in the world – and the second highest level of stunting. A diet of little more than tortillas does permanent damage and helps create a cycle of poverty and suffering. So a proper diet, which the Pueblo a Pueblo project is inculcating, is the first step in breaking the cycle.

It is distressing to note that Pueblo a Pueblo is still struggling to build appropriate relationships with local government. Guatemala is, by most economic analyses, rich enough to prevent chronic malnutrition. With the exception of Haiti, other Latin and Central American countries have significantly reduced child hunger – but even in Haiti the rate of stunting is half that of Guatemala. This points to a failure of government at a local and national level.

We went on to see one of the five schools which Pueblo a Pueblo had helped to relocate and rebuild. Ossie and Veronica were most impressed by the remains of the buildings still half buried in the mud, which by now was like concrete, and the steel beams twisted by the mud flow. The results of the destruction were still very apparent almost everywhere.

Two days later we went off to visit the GFA's long-term charity partner BPD, whom we had visited when we last came over in 2006. One of the administrators and co-ordinators came along to help with translations. Once again the children were thrilled to be allowed to travel in the back of their truck in the same way as all the local children. We first went to Chuaquenun, where the GFA had funded the whole backpack programme. The efficacy of the work that had been done was obvious. The improvements in health and fitness of everyone, but particularly the children, was easy to see. Also the number of children, and especially girls, attending and benefiting from education had significantly increased – all of which spoke of long-term genuine improved chances for health and happiness for all in the village.

But there were also other subtle differences we were really glad to see. We were introduced to two orphans, little girls whose mother had died a year or so before. Because of the increased food prosperity in the village they were cared for by the villagers and were thriving – a few years ago this would not have been possible as there would not have been any surplus.

I think our children really benefit from the first-hand knowledge they gain of the realities of life for rural Guatemalans, which their birth families are, and how with the right sort of respectful and targeted support things can be drastically improved. By getting an untrammelled view of the lives of ordinary indigenous Guatemalans they are able to visualise the lives of their birth families to create realistic understanding, and thus empathy for the situation that led to their relinquishments and subsequent adoptions. This does not make it less difficult or the loss less painful, but it is easier for them to imagine the pressures and situations that surrounded their early lives.

The final part of the journey was going down towards the Honduran border where we had planned to spend time with Ossie's birth family and go over the border briefly to visit Copan, one of the greatest Mayan sites. We drove down very early in the morning and met "S" at the holiday complex where we were going to stay. We had booked two cabins, one for us and one for our birth family; the complex was full of outdoor pools with slides and fountains, interspersed with other recreational facilities like mini golf and badminton and volleyball courts.

We all stood outside on the street and waited for "M" and her family to arrive. Suddenly there was a huge cloud of dust filling the air as a bus swerved off onto the verge and seconds later lurched back onto the road. As the dust settled a group emerged holding hands. Slightly hesitantly we went to meet them. There were a lot of hopes and dreams invested in this meeting, and yet there was also an element of fear and uncertainty. Had they grown away from us – had something come between us that the regular exchange of letters and photos had concealed – would they make demands we would struggle to meet?

For whatever reason, and I would always ascribe it to the amazing flexibility and generosity of "M" and her husband and children, we just "got on" as we had done before. They were in surroundings far more alien for them than for us, we were more travelled and used to a wider range of places and cultures. We had the benefit of having had Ossie in our family for fourteen years – while they had been missing him. And yet they fitted in, and graciously accepted the gifts we had brought, including swimming kit and towels for all of them. The children just had fun. They splashed in the water – it turned out that all three of Ossie's half-brothers are strong swimmers, having learned to swim in the rivers out of whose beds other family members were digging gravel. They slid down the slides, they played mini golf and played soccer on the courts.

Ossie clearly had genuine ties to his half-brothers, Veronica built a very strong bond with the youngest, who seemed to reciprocate it, and they spent a lot of time draped all over each other. Ossie, Veronica and the boys ran everywhere, luxuriating in their abilities and skills and communicating as much through touch and gesture as through language.

One of "M"'s sisters had come along with her son who was disabled – I never quite understood how it had started, but the treatment he had received for his spine had made him worse, and now he needs to be carried and supported all the time. He and his mother enjoyed relaxing in the pools where the water enabled him to float, weightlessly.

Elly, "S" and I sat down with "M" and her husband and chatted. Even though we lived such different lives we were able to talk about everyday things and, of course, we were joined by the love for the son we shared. Learning from our experience with BPD, we arranged for them to get, with "S"'s organisation's help, a water filter system and a stove to make their house safer. We were already sponsoring Ossie's half-brothers through school, although they obviously found it hard going, and we discussed the value of education and that it should be continued. We talked about how "M"'s husband's job as a truck driver took him away from home for long periods, and how it was harder for "M" to look after the boys on her own. We talked about elderly parents and the issues relating to their care.

The hardest part was talking about Ossie. "M" is an amazingly strong woman but one can see that it is still hard for her to see Ossie and imagine how different things might have been. She always reiterates her thanks for our love and care and for being *compadres*, but what can you say to the woman who has given you a most precious son? Thank you is simply not adequate.

After "S" had left we stayed together at the resort for a night and a day before dropping "M" and her partner and family off at the nearest point on the road to their home. After saying our goodbyes, promising to come back as soon as possible, lots of hugs and kisses, they all trudged off through the fields and under the trees heading for their house. We climbed back into the people carrier and set off for Copan. At first there was silence as we each dealt with our own thoughts – and felt a mixture of sadness on parting from Ossie's birth family and relief that things seemed to have gone so well for Ossie and Veronica. We reflected on how different our lives were, planned what we might do to help more, mused on the injustices of the Guatemalan political and economic systems and how lucky we are as a family to be able to have everything we have – especially our *familia*.

As we walked about the incredible ruins of one of the greatest flowerings of the Mayan civilization, Copan, we were able to talk – probably to the detriment of our ability to take in where we were and what lay before us.

Teenagers – especially those in early adolescence – live very much in the intensity of the moment. Their world often does not extend beyond family, friends, school, sports or other peer activities. When these close props are shaken or they move away from them, underlying issues of adolescent self-esteem and identity (and for some children loss) can shake them to the core. When they do, it is our role as parents to walk with them through their darkest fears and guide them towards healthy coping strategies. We have to be able to talk to them about handling painful feelings and dealing with seemingly unbearable situations.

While walking through those amazing inspirational surroundings (and doing a lot of exhausted sitting on carved stones) we were able to talk about our unfaltering presence in Ossie's and Veronica's lives – that there was nothing that they could ever do that would stop us from loving them; that we could not be disappointed or discouraged by the essential them. That whilst we might not be happy with specific behaviours, there was nothing they could do or feel that we could not get through together; that we are all linked with this amazing place and we are all part of our *familia*.

It was an exhausted but exhilarated family that returned home late that night to our rented house in Antigua where the Easter celebrations were still going on. In the little time we had left we packed in as much as we could. Elly and the children climbed a live volcano and enjoyed marshmallows roasted over an open lava vent. More shopping, more processions, more photos – it all rushed past in a blur and in seemingly no time at all we were on the plane home.

The hallway is full of suitcases and bags again. Shoes litter the floor and coats are strewn around. In the kitchen the kettle is gurgling away, ready to make that most vital potion – the first cup of proper English tea after you come home. We are home again and as the days pass we are able to reflect on the trip and how it has affected us. We think about what we have learned and we look forward. We look forward with hope to continuing our journey as a family and part of our *familia* – building on our roots in Guatemala, England, Croatia, Scotland and Japan; keeping our links with the adoption community; developing our friendships and above all being happy and content within ourselves.

PART 3

Green: the colour of hope

As I look to the future there are still many unanswered questions in my mind: How can I help our children to be happy? How can I help them to appreciate being part of a multiracial family? How will our family experience adoption in the future? One of the issues is the lack of real information and advice.

There is a paucity of empirical research on transracial or intercountry adoptions. Most of the publicly available work is scattered, fragmentary and narrowly defined.

Many of the studies are old and do not show how the social context of multiculturalism has changed. Generally they focus on the adaptation of the child to the new family. Few, if any, ever asked how well the family adapted to its new multiracial, multicultural identity.

There are still traces of the troubled history of adoption in Britain in the literature. Our society still seems to value biological connections more highly and casts shadows of doubt on adoptive parenting. Most psychologically oriented studies are interested in the problems of adoptive families, based on those who have approached mental health or other professionals for help with their children.

However, the existing studies on intercountry adoptees do paint an optimistic picture.★ They report overall positive outcomes, with only about 10 per cent presenting serious problems; the vast majority of adoptees interviewed showed positive self-esteem. Professor Rutter's large-scale Romanian project in the UK provided evidence of the amazing resilience and capacity to heal of the most damaged children.

But there remains a lack of positive parenting information and advice. Most studies of intercountry adoptive families concentrate on the effects of what is missing. I want to read how the families became different as they developed a multicultural, multiracial identity and their children grew through to adulthood.

I want to make sure that I find a way to ensure that our children's loss and the events of their early lives are not minimised. I need to find ways to acknowledge that there was a time in their lives when it felt that they did not matter, that they were not important to someone. I have to let them know that I accept that their beginnings, marked by relinquishment, separation and loss, will forever be with them, and that they will need support and affirmation to be able to be gentle and kind to themselves.

At the same time it is not fair to cocoon them. When they go out into society on their own, as they are increasingly doing, they need to be fully equipped to navigate our racially charged world. I need to help them to anticipate how the world will treat them as people of colour. I owe it to them to empower them with the language, the skills and the permission to talk about "race", racism and white privilege. I have no illusions that they will be afforded the same privileges, benefits and unearned rights that I have been, and I challenge myself to see the world through the eyes of our children.

★ Various studies by Van IJzendoorn and Juffer in recent years cover the area well, as does Rutter *et al's* study of Romanian adopters.

When I was a rugby player, along with my fellow denizens of the front row, we knew that with good training and the right technique we would be able to not only survive, but to thrive on the physicality and adrenaline-fuelled joy of the game. We knew that, like Henry V's band of brothers, we would

> ...imitate the action of the tiger
> Stiffen the sinews, summon up the blood
> Disguise fair nature with hard-favour'd rage.

and get through all obstacles to reach our goals – 'doors not walls' was how we used to express it.

It is similar for our children. Their schools, their social groups, the neighbourhood, and in time their places of work all offer opportunities for either doors or walls. Sometimes the walls will be obstructions built from other people's unwillingness, complacency, ignorance, or secure positions of privilege. Sometimes the walls come from fear or self-imposed barriers.

It is not enough for our children to know that we love them unconditionally. We have to help them find the right words, the effective strategies they need to find the doors and open them.

Unfortunately there will never be a shortage of walls to overcome. I just want Ossie and Veronica to be confident to know that there is no wall without a door to let them move forward and, most importantly, they don't have to do it alone. I want them to know that we, their parents, really want to learn what it takes to be their ally.

But issues of "race" or other prejudice are not the only concerns. Too much emphasis on the specific aspects of our children's heritage and history will blind us to the wider task of becoming parents.

As we all move forward as a family there are parenting skills I need to develop. I am often reminded of the Yusuf Islam (Cat Stevens) song *Father and Son* and the words: *'from the moment I could talk I was ordered to listen'*. It is not only essential to keep talking, but even more essential to keep listening to our children. They have really valuable messages to give us, not the least of which is that they are involved in all of their own lives, and they want us to be involved, but under their terms. "Do as I say" no longer works. Our actions and beliefs have to match our values and those we wish them to absorb. I have to make sure that I not only meet this standard, but that I communicate it as well.

I also have to give them more and more opportunities to learn and grow, which can be quite scary for a Mum and a Dad. It may be natural for teens to stick with people they identify as being most like themselves, in groups they feel most comfortable with, but it is also important for them to go outside their comfort zones and broaden their social circles. I hope that Ossie and Veronica will go further and take up causes they feel strongly about, become active in their communities and feel empowered to fight for change.

How are we going to achieve all these wonderful things? Right now I really don't know – but 'doors not walls' means that there must be a way, we just have to find it together.

I have written this in a spirit of hope. Hope that by sharing some of our story others may benefit and be informed. Hope that attitudes to intercountry and transracial adoption will move forward and that the structures and institutions that create barriers are overcome. Hope that more children, wherever they may be, for whom adoption is their only route to a family, will find one – and that they will also be able to keep their *familia*.

Adoption has brought me my treasured family and I have felt joy, unconstrained, but I will always remember that we are also part of a wider *familia*.

Postscript from Veronica

I was relinquished when I was 10 days old. I didn't actually get to England until I was 18 months old. It was never a secret that I was adopted and I've always known that my Mum and Dad love me very much and want me to be happy. They have always given me every chance to explore where I originate from. We, as a family, have spoken freely and openly about the adoption process from when they first saw me.

We went to Guatemala to try to find my birth mother and family. Sadly we reached a dead end. My brother was luckier than me. He found his mother. It was very emotional because she said what was hers was mine and what was mine was hers. I knew I was part of her family just as she is part of ours.

I was really unhappy because I didn't get to see my birth mother – that really hurts. I would like to go back to Guatemala again soon and try again.

The most important thing is for kids to feel safe to find out about themselves and know that they are loved. If I didn't know that I was loved then I would think they were doing it out of pity. I hate people pitying me.

Social workers say parents who adopt from another country can't show their children about culture and origins. Well, just look at me. I learn each day about where I am from and all the good and bad things about that. They care that I have all this information because then I can make my own choices freely. Plus if I want to, I can help others and I do help other people because that's who I am.

Adoption is sad and happy at the same time because you get a new family but you can lose one too. Being adopted does not mean you have to miss out on anything – and sometimes you get extra.